THE JOHN RYLANDS UNIVERSITY LIBRARY

assessing reading 2:

changing practice in classrooms

international perspectives on reading assessment

edited by martin coles and rhonda jenkins

ROUTLEDGE

ASSESSING READING 2:
CHANGING PRACTICE IN CLASSROOMS

This book, along with its companion volume *Assessing Reading 1: Theory and Practice*, was originally conceived as the major outcome from an international seminar on reading assessment in England. It focuses directly on the classroom, on the challenges individual teachers face in classroom-based assessment, and how these challenges have been and are being met in a range of international contexts.

Each chapter reports classroom-based explorations of new approaches to reading assessment. So the book as a whole offers a wide range of examples of alternative assessments, including portfolio assessment, diagnostic assessment, self-assessment and reading interviews. The writers also continue the discussion in the first volume of issues such as how alternative approaches to assessment might be integrated into the curriculum, and how these approaches may be used to serve information needs at state or national level.

The book aims to increase collective professional knowledge by sharing international perspectives and practices and in doing this to help teachers become more effective and feel more confident in using new approaches to reading assessment.

Martin Coles is Senior Lecturer in Education at the University of Nottingham. **Rhonda Jenkins** is a freelance publishing adviser.

ASSESSING READING 2:

CHANGING PRACTICE IN CLASSROOMS

International Perspectives on Reading
Assessment

*Edited by Martin Coles
and Rhonda Jenkins*

London and New York

AO-IU.

(DW5J9)

375·42

C365

JOHN RYLANDS
UNIVERSITY
LIBRARY OF
MANCHESTER

First published 1998
by Routledge
11 New Fetter Lane, London EC4P 4EE

Simultaneously published in the USA and Canada
by Routledge
29 West 35th Street, New York, NY 10001

© 1998 Martin Coles and Rhonda Jenkins, selection and editorial matter;
individual chapters © their contributors

Typeset in Garamond by
Florencetype Ltd, Stoodleigh, Devon

Printed and bound in Great Britain by
Creative Print and Design (Wales), Ebbw Vale

All rights reserved. No part of this book may be reprinted or reproduced or
utilized in any form or by any electronic, mechanical, or other means, now
known or hereafter invented, including photocopying and recording, or in
any information storage or retrieval system, without permission in writing
from the publishers.

British Library Cataloguing in Publication Data
A catalogue record for this book is available from the British Library

Library of Congress Cataloging in Publication Data
A catalogue record for this book has been requested

ISBN   0–415–14895–2
0–415–14896–0 (pbk)

CONTENTS

FIGURES

CONTRIBUTORS

Mary Bailey	University of Nottingham, England
Martin Coles	University of Nottingham, England
Alan Dewar	Dukeries Community College, Nottinghamshire, England
Chris Foster	Kingsway Junior School, Kingsway, Nottinghamshire, England
Graham Frater	Formerly a member of Her Majesty's Inspectorate, England
Mike Hamlin	Greenwood Dale Comprehensive School, Nottingham, England
Colin Harrison	University of Nottingham, England
Louise Hayward	St Andrews College, Glasgow, Scotland
James V. Hoffman	University of Texas, USA
Rhonda Jenkins	First Steps Consultancy Unit, England
Sharon McKool	University of Texas, USA
Myles Myers	Michigan State University, USA
P. David Pearson	Michigan State University, USA
Nancy L. Roser	University of Texas, USA
William Rutherford	University of Texas, USA
Terry Salinger	American Institutes for Research, Washington DC, USA
Patricia G. Smith	Assessment Research Centre, Royal Melbourne Institute of Technology, Victoria, Australia
Elizabeth Spalding	University of Kentucky, USA
Ernie Spencer	Scottish Office, Education and Industry Department
Susan Streckor	University of Texas, USA
Jo Worthy	University of Texas, USA

INTRODUCTION

Martin Coles and Rhonda Jenkins

This book, and its companion volume *Assessing Reading 1: Theory and Practice*, were originally conceived as the major outcomes from an invited international seminar on reading assessment held in England in 1995. The seminar had been proposed for two main reasons. First, at the time of the seminar, the assessment of reading in England and Wales was in turmoil. The government had taken over reading assessment, but it had dismissed a number of groups which were originally funded to write national tests, and recruited others whose efforts were not fully implemented due to a national boycott of tests by teachers. There was an urgent concern within the UK that government initiatives on assessment did not so absorb the attention and energy of those concerned with reading assessment that a vacuum would be created in relation to a broader consideration of principles, theory and practice. Second, a similar pattern of national anxieties over standards and reassessment of approaches to testing was evident in other countries, and within those countries many significant changes and innovations were under way.

In Australia and in Scotland, innovative practices were being introduced within national curriculum assessment, and in the USA literacy professionals had begun the search for new paradigms within which to address the urgent issues of assessment, both within the National Reading Research Center initiatives and the National Standards project, and within the wider reading assessment community. The seminar, which was titled New Paradigms in Reading Assessment, sought to set up an international forum for pooling information on these initiatives in reading assessment, to bring together the work of internationally recognized academics in the reading field in order to share information in this rapidly expanding area, to advance and clarify theories of reading assessment, to locate areas for new research initiatives, to reduce duplication of effort, and to disseminate evidence of reliability, validity and utility for potential users in other professional contexts.

The chapters in this book have been written as an outcome of the discussions at the original seminars, and subsequently. It is one of two complementary volumes. The companion volume, *Assessing Reading 1:*

Theory and Practice, addresses theoretical and research issues, especially national and state level approaches to reading assessment. This volume focuses more directly on the classroom. In particular it focuses on the challenges individual teachers face in portfolio and authentic assessment and how these have been and are being met in a range of approaches internationally. Both books are distinctive in their international orientation. This volume provides evidence and descriptions of innovative practice from Australia, England, Scotland and the USA.

To provide a book which charts key practical issues in reading assessment in three continents is extraordinarily difficult, not only because the culture of assessment varies greatly between countries, but also because the discourse of assessment varies so greatly. Yet it is imperative that we learn from each other's theory and practice, in order to avoid duplication of effort and, if possible, duplication of error. To do this, however, the editors felt that it would be necessary to have each chapter edited twice, from a national and an international perspective, where necessary cross-referencing and rewriting to make the argument clearer to colleagues from a different assessment culture and discourse community. This process has taken time, but the editors were fortunate in having authors who cooperated fully and cheerfully in this enterprise, and it is the hope of both authors and editors that this process will have been successful in producing a volume which advances practice in its field in three continents.

The content and structure of this book

Many of the issues which are addressed in the present book are developed from its companion volume, which also has an international editorial team, Colin Harrison of England and Terry Salinger from the USA. The intention of the two volumes is to bring together the work of professionals from different countries to provide complementary information, discussion and advice about reading assessment. The aim is to connect theory, research and practice from different cultural contexts. The authors of the various chapters, all professionally concerned with reading assessment, are committed to the view that we can all make better progress in practice if there is thoughtful cross-cultural exchange of ideas. Then we will begin to avoid assumptions that are unique to and driven by our cultural situation.

Each of the chapters reports classroom-based explorations of new approaches to reading assessment, and so the book as a whole offers a wide range of illustrations of alternative assessments, including portfolio assessment, diagnostic assessment, self-assessment and reading interviews. The authors also continue the discussion of such important issues as how alternative approaches to assessment might be integrated into the curriculum and how these approaches may be used to serve the information needs at state or national level.

The emphasis in this book is on describing practice, but this practice is not without a foundation in theory. The companion volume offers clear pointers indicating why the practical approaches which are offered for consideration here are theoretically sound and can be fully supported by recent advances in theory.

Chapter 1 briefly offers a summary of this theory and introduces the other chapters which comprise this book. In these nine chapters there are accounts that provide information on practice within various systems. All chapters are descriptive of what is deemed promising practice. The voices in the different chapters may diverge culturally and authors may have different types of professional experience, but the stances taken, and the understandings implicit in the practice, coincide with each other.

The framework we have selected for ordering the chapters attempts to offer coherence. Even though the chapters deal with different systems in different countries some strands overlap and interrelate. The chapters in Part 1 offer accounts of changes in reading assessment at a level above that of an individual classroom or school.

The links between curriculum practice and policy implementation are made in Terry Salinger's chapter. It focuses on how changes to reading assessment practice were brought about in one school district from the perspective of the initial cadre of teachers who planned and motivated that change, devised a 'portfolio' assessment system, developed scoring mechanisms, and implemented the portfolio in their own classrooms. The chapter describes the system in operation and identifies those decision points that were crucial to the successful implementation of the portfolio assessment system and the factors that have jeopardized its effectiveness.

Louise Hayward and Ernie Spencer describe 'Taking a Closer Look at Reading', a package of diagnostic procedures to help teachers assess reading in day to day classroom work. This project is a national initiative in Scotland which emphasizes the teacher's crucial role in diagnosis and teaching for reading development, and the need for supporting the teacher in becoming more confident and effective in this role. The Scottish project focuses on helping teachers use daily observational and interview procedures to clarify pupils' strengths and weaknesses. There is in this system an integration of assessment, recording, evaluation and planning, and learning and teaching. There is a formative use of standard assessment criteria, an occasional summative evaluation based on holistic judgement, and a national testing system which is used to confirm the teacher judgements.

From Texas comes a description of the PALM project (Primary Assessment of Language Arts and Mathematics) by Jo Worthy, James Hoffman, Nancy Roser, William Rutherford, Sharon McKool and Susan Strecker. This chapter explains how the project developed the processes of an alternative assessment plan in selected first-grade classrooms in the Austin Independent School District. The chapter shows how to document reading growth from the very earliest stages of literacy development. The ultimate aim is to develop an assessment system for the early grades that will serve the development interests of children, the needs of teachers and the policy needs of public representatives. It allows every teacher to document progress for every child, providing data to support and inform decisions about daily teaching and data which can be used by administrators. The work tries to address the tension there is between wanting an assessment system that is commonly understood and interpreted, and allowing the system to stay open to improvement and adaptation to classroom needs.

In the final chapter of Part 1, David Pearson, Liz Spalding and Miles Myers describe the recent experience of teachers and investigators developing and refining alternative assessment tools which document the growth and accomplishment in reading for both school-based and external constituencies. The project, now well known in America simply as New Standards, is committed to nothing less than the reform of America's schools through the development of high standards for all students in science, maths and the English language arts and rigorous assessment systems that will allow all stakeholders in the enterprise to monitor progress towards achieving those high standards. The authors explain how they see this as now the major challenge – to develop assessment frameworks which maintain a balance between the priorities of the classroom and the imperatives of what is called in America 'high stakes assessment'.

Part 2 takes a more direct focus on the classroom, on the challenges individual teachers face in portfolio and authentic assessment, and how these have been and are being met in a range of approaches. Many of the chapters in this section draw on the 'voices' of children and teachers to demonstrate new approaches to reading assessment in action.

Colin Harrison, Mary Bailey and Chris Foster examine the potential of some often-neglected approaches to the problem of seeking evidence of reading achievement, by reporting case studies based on interviews, book reports on leisure reading, and tape-recordings made by students. They ask a crucial question about the basis on which we should consider innovation or change in assessment and suggest that there are some first principles on which we can build, and which lead to the notion of *responsive assessment*, some aspects of which are illustrated in the case studies.

From Australia Pat Smith reports on one integrated assessment package which uses classroom-based assessment that gives the teachers a crucial and substantial role, but which can also produce aggregated data for non-local purposes. Her chapter explores the complex relationship between learning, teaching, assessing and reporting by considering the work of one 11-year-old-boy, Maxwell Pogonowski. A 'Literacy Profile' of Max's work and thinking gives a sense of Max's lively development as a reader. This chapter explains how such literacy profiles enable teachers to embody all the best principles of assessment and reporting practices by encouraging them to use multiple methods of observation and by providing criterion-referenced descriptions.

In England, teachers have accumulated over thirty years' experience in administering and calibrating assessments in reading and writing at secondary level within a system in which teacher judgement of pupil performance was, until very recently, the basis for national assessment at the end of secondary education. Mike Hamlin describes this careful system of school, local and regional agreement trials, trial marking (grading) procedures, inter-school assessment and national review panels. He notes the changes which have recently occurred which mean a move away from what came to be known as '100 per cent coursework' examinations and explains the practical measures which teachers are taking to try to maintain examination assessment which encourages wide reading and an opportunity to discuss what is being read.

Alan Dewar sets out to see if useful information about pupils' reading can be gained from interviewing them about drafts of their own writing. He discusses the value and purposes of such information and the relationships between information gained in this way and the other kinds of information we can gather about pupils' reading. The starting point of this exploration is the recognition that, although reading and writing are often separated for assessment purposes, in practice they are so closely related as to be almost inseparable, a point made in detail in the chapter by Harrison, Bailey and Foster in this volume.

Finally Graham Frater draws on his extensive experience as one of Her Majesty's Inspectors of Schools in England, and on a survey he undertook for the Basic Skills Agency in England into the provision for Special Educational Needs (SEN) in secondary schools in England to make a case for new paradigms of literacy assessment for pupils with special needs in the secondary school and for new courses of action based upon them.

The whole book aims, then, to increase collective professional knowledge by sharing international perspectives and practices and, in doing this, to help teachers become more effective and feel more confident in using new approaches to reading assessment.

Part I

TEACHERS CHANGING THE SYSTEM

1

ASSESSING READING

Changing practice

Martin Coles

Learning to read and write is perceived to be important across countries and cultures. Literacy is central to the curriculum of most educational systems and standards of literacy are of major interest to parents, pupils, politicians and the media in most western societies. Since issues to do with the assessment of reading are not confined to national boundaries it must be right, in considering reading assessment, to be aware of what is happening in different countries. The different chapters in the book have this is common: they explain the assessment cultures within which teachers in different systems operate and they describe the distinctiveness of practice in different classrooms. So this short chapter sets out to provide a context for the following chapters, which describe practice in different systems, in terms of those reading assessment issues which are common to all.

The work of colleagues in the different countries represented in this book suggests that shared understandings are gradually emerging of ways forward in reading assessment. Inevitably there will be different emphases from country to country and ongoing theoretical debate that will have implications for classroom practice. Different sites and different countries have developed particular professional expertise, particularly in terms of classroom-based approaches to reading assessment and the cultural perspective they bring to the dialogue. This book is a recognition of the importance of these different cultural perspectives and types of expertise. But despite cultural differences there are common issues and debates. For instance, although working definitions and terminology for assessment practices differ across locations, the central purposes and understandings are very often the same. For example, portfolio assessment in its various forms and under different headings in different countries has as a constant the aim of supporting instruction and bringing assessment methods into line with the curriculum. Putting into practice what is learned from the practice of others is not always easy, but there are here clear signals to ways forward in reading assessment.

Why move away from traditional tests?

Traditionally the assessment of reading progress has been made through the administration of published standardized tests. Despite the advent of performance-based assessment, the most common form of assessment in those countries which have contributed to this book remains standardized, commercially produced paper and pencil tests. Although formal statistical evidence is unavailable, the experience of those gathered at the seminars which were the catalyst for this book suggests that most schools still use standardized tests as the base on which to make judgements about children's reading abilities. These tests are either multiple choice, single-correct answer formats, word reading, or sentence reading tests. Some may be designed around a short information-laden story followed by a set of questions which require the respondent to draw inferences from the facts in the passage. Certainly the assessment activities which children have to suffer are not decreasing – as well as standardized tests there are also reading scheme tests, national (and in some countries local) testing, individual school tests and teacher-made tests.

Often this testing has very little to do with helping the individual child and a lot to do with accountability within the school system. Politicians particularly are concerned that education 'delivers' in a way that will support the economic ambitions of the country and they, as well as many members of the public, believe that test scores are a good indicator of 'value for money' and a clear signpost to standards of achievement. But of course this assessment directly affects what teachers teach and what children learn. The most direct influence comes when teachers and pupils take time out of the curriculum to prepare for tests, but there are other less obvious effects, for instance, when educational publishers design their materials in order to stress the close ties between their publication and the most widely used tests. Here the 'backwash effect' on the curriculum is particularly pernicious. And as teachers receive more and more pressure to raise test scores, tests come to have a greater hold on the curriculum.

The problem in a lot of this assessment is the practice of measuring reading rather than analysing it. Treating reading as a single measurable accomplishment masks the complexity of the process and leaves argument about the teaching of reading up in the air. Standardized tests have not yet been devised which cover all the aspects of the very complex process involved in reading and children's reading is not improved simply by being measured, any more than babies grow as a result of being regularly weighed. Reading 'scores' or 'levels' very often appear to provide indications of progression but are really of little help to the child or the teacher. And the entire enterprise is often completely meaningless to the child.

One other major problem is that formal assessments traditionally evaluate pupils on a normative measure, that is, by comparing pupils' performances with each other and evaluating their performance against the mean. The inevitable result is that only a few pupils do well, the large majority are judged to be around the average, and the rest are below average. And rarely in this banding of pupils into ability sets is information acquired which is of genuine use to teachers. How can teachers respond to a simple score? If it is a number all teachers can try to do is make it larger. In these circumstances teaching to the test is the only option. But teaching to the test does not necessarily improve reading competence. A person might memorize the multiplication tables and perform well on various simple tests, exactly as would someone who knows the rules of arithmetic, but a good performance here does not, of course, show that this person knows the rules. The same is true for reading. Competence in 'real' reading situations is the information which has most relevance.

Perhaps we have been satisfied with standardized test scores in the past partly because the term 'reading' implies a single piece of behaviour. So there is often a lack of understanding that there is no simple answer to the question 'what is progress in reading?'. Too often in the past we have been happy to commit the numerical fallacy of a score! We assign readers to a number as if numbers represent equidistant points in reading progress/development, a process which does not acknowledge that readers develop in different ways and at different paces. Language development, we now understand, is not a linear sequence. Rather it is a process of refining competence as different aspects of development are returned to with increasing sophistication. It follows that there is no easy way of assessing reading progress either. Now that we are beginning to understand the complexity of the reading process it is essential that our assessment procedures reflect this knowledge. It is no longer acceptable to administer a reading test once a year in order to monitor a pupil's progress in reading and to believe this gives anything like an adequate picture of the child as reader.

A paradigm shift

The two volumes in this series call for a paradigm shift, a move away from the old models of reading assessment. What is this paradigm shift? Dissatisfaction with the old allows you to stand in a new place to consider a way forward. New models in these papers are attempts to move forward, to explore new forms of assessment at both policy/system and classroom level.

Historical movement is towards national testing, but this movement is in tension with a new movement to align the assessment instruments with ordinary classroom tasks, moving away from static, numerical measures to descriptions of reading ability, a move from quantitative to qualitative data. The chapters in this book are evidence and descriptions both of what can be done, for instance, by placing emphasis on positive achievement, and of a common understanding that national testing cannot take into account the relationship between teacher and child.

Traditional tests are an accountant's measure. They reflect the capitalist ledger of profit and loss. They attempt to contain complexity by the application of the tools of rationality. Machine-like precision is aimed for, apparently bound by the rules of rational procedure. But we now understand that a single attachment to systematic, scientific reality is a dangerous deception. The world, and people, cannot be *simply* measured. The paradigm shift in reading assessment, then, reflects what is happening in a variety of fields of knowledge. We are thinking again about the old world of belief in solid scientific facts and the desire to eliminate uncertainty and ambivalence. There is now a general acceptance of the view that our observations depend on our assumptions and those assumptions are connected with power positions and world-views. So it is with reading assessment. The very act of giving an assessment is a demonstration of power. Pearson, DeStefano and Garcia (1995: 18) explain this problem and the way forward from it:

> One individual tells the other what to read, how to respond, how much time to take. One insinuates a sense of greater power because of greater knowledge (i.e. possession of the right answers). The brightest ray of hope emanating from our recent candidates for assessment reform is their public disposition. If assessment becomes a completely open process in all its phases from conception to development to interpretation, then at least the hidden biases will become more visible and at best everyone will have a clearer sense of what counts in our schools.

The dominance of natural science in our society and the rise of technology sometimes seems to squeeze out concern with real-life individuals. Aspects of industrial production, such as uniformity and standardization, have become common features of modern life. Often tasks are broken down into component parts, timed and checked in order to maximize productivity and profit. The discourses of this type of thinking are tabulation, classification and processing. Until very recently the debate about school standards and progress in reading was trapped in this vocabulary. Now, in the field of reading assessment, as in many others, we are moving forward towards a concern for the individual and taking an interest in the local rather than the universal.

New models of assessment

This book, then, does not concern itself with large-scale national assessment but with new local models where, for instance, pupils' classroom work and their reflections on that work provide a richer and truer picture of competencies than do traditional tests.

Since assessing reading requires a sample of reading performance the choice is between an observation of that performance in context, or the prediction of actual performance from a surrogate activity. Put like this it seems odd that we have for so long relied on the latter. Quick and easy tests which, for instance, indicate how well children recognize individual words under strange conditions, do not begin to match up to what we know of literacy and literacy learning. In such tests the vastly complex process of reading is reduced to a simple uni-dimensional linearity, so that the children, classes and schools can be placed in rank order. How can such a test tell a teacher about children's values and habits which are also part of reading development? Reading is, after all, not simply an instrumental activity, it is also a recreational and imaginative experience which engages a reader at the affective level as well as the cognitive. The new models of assessment potentially allow us to see children operating at full potential, engaged in tasks which command their commitment. And they allow space to ensure that the business of assessment involves children in reflecting on their own learning, both as contributors to an evaluation and as receivers of those evaluations. So children are not to be treated 'as laboratory "subjects" – producers of data at other people's requests, to be used for other people's purposes' (Dombey 1991). The TGAT report (National Curriculum Task Group on Assessment and Testing) in England stresses that the assessment process itself should be part of the educational process, continually providing teachers with feedback on the success of their teaching strategies and information which they can use in making future teaching plans:

> The assessment process itself should not determine what is taught and learned. It should be the servant and not the master of the curriculum. Yet it should not simply be a bolt-on addition at the end. Rather it should be an integral part of the educational process, continually providing both 'feedback' and 'feedforward'. It therefore needs to be incorporated systematically into teaching strategies and practices at all levels.
>
> (DES, 1988)

In other words, the central purpose of assessment is to obtain knowledge that can be used to help the pupil. All other purposes are secondary. This government report, the spirit of which is gradually being lost in revisions to the national testing regime in England, endorses the need for methods of assessment to be incorporated into normal classroom activities. In this way they are more likely to reflect the actual achievements of the pupils; that is, the closer assessment procedures are to everyday classroom activities, the more valid the results will be.

We must not, though, assume that performance/classroom assessment is unproblematic. The very fact that it has both evaluative and instructional purposes means it is inauthentic in one sense. Authenticity can be a false notion – very few school language tasks reflect the world outside school and to try to solve one aspect of this problem by offering assessment tasks to children without telling them 'this is assessment' is ethically questionable.

Finally, it is important to realize that a full performance assessment is a complex interpretative act. It places the teacher at the heart of an interactive process of talking and listening, whereas traditional performance tests, although unrepresentative of the reading process, can be quick and easily administered. In the past the logistical advantages of the 'test' have won the day in schools. Ease of management has taken precedence over usefulness and doing the best for the individual pupil. But assessment programmes which view the teacher simply as a technician who administers tests, deskill teachers. New forms of assessment make it clear that assessment skills required of teachers should be an integral part of the professional skills of a reading teacher. Since the purpose of this type of assessment is to improve the child's performance, it is the teacher who is at the heart of the assessment process simply because the teacher is most directly involved with the child. In most teaching teachers are in any case continuously making judgements about how the pupils are progressing. It is a process of sense-making embedded in the whole fabric of meaning and activity in the classroom. Teacher assessment of reading might, in this context, be seen as analogous to the process of reading itself, i.e. the teacher 'reads' the reader taking account of the text (what the reader is saying) and the context (the knowledge of the reader and the setting in which the reading is taking place).

In the field of reading assessment, as in many others, it is often difficult to get experts to agree. In this book, however, shared understandings are evident. A summary of the principles which provide the foundations for the chapters in this book might be:

- at the heart of any assessment should be promotion of the pupil's learning;
- use 'real' tasks similar to basic curriculum tasks and use multiple pieces of evidence that reflect the progress and development of the reader;
- recognize uncertainty – reading assessment is a nuanced exercise;
- describe the competencies that readers have developed, what they can do, rather than simply a comparison with other readers;
- describe progress in a way which has the same meaning for the readers themselves, other teachers, parents and other interested parties;
- see assessment as integral to professional development and curriculum change.

Concluding remarks

In England, Christian Schiller was a charismatic Inspector of Schools between 1924 and 1955. An excerpt from one of his papers is quoted at length to end this short introductory chapter. His words, spoken over fifty years ago, eloquently express a view of reading assessment which lies behind each of the chapters in this book, a view which is only now becoming powerful in practice:

> They say that no one truly sees his own face. This mercy of nature comes from the fact that reflections in the mirror show partial pictures which are flat: they cannot show an object in the round. To see an object in the round it must be observed as a whole. . . . The skills of young children show reflection of their attainment, but they do not show attainment in the round. To see their attainment in the round we must observe it in their way of living. . . . Mary Smith's score in the reading test is a measure of her skill in turning black marks into sounds. To see her attainment in the round we must observe *how* she reads. With what quality of understanding does she read? How fully has she experienced the enjoyment of reading? For how long does she remain interested in a book? What sort of book does she like to read? How pleasantly can she read aloud? How much can she appreciate the reading aloud of others. Does she ever read at home? And so on. Such observation will begin to show Mary's attainment in the round . . . but such observation is not easy.
>
> (Griffin-Beale 1979)

References

DES (1988) *National Curriculum Task Group on Assessment and Testing: A Report*, London: Department of Education and Science.

Dombey, H. (1991) 'The satable and the unsattable: giving our children the assessment in literacy that they deserve', in C. Harrison and E. Ashworth (eds) *Celebrating Literacy: Defending Literacy*, Oxford: Blackwell.

Griffin-Beale, C. (ed.) (1979) *Christian Schiller: In His Own Words*, London: A.C. Black.

Pearson, D., DeStefano, L. and García, G.E. (1995) 'Dilemmas in performance assessment', paper presented at the New Paradigms in Reading Assessment seminar, Nottingham University, UK.

2

DEVELOPING AN EARLY LITERACY PORTFOLIO FOR DISTRICT-WIDE USE

Terry Salinger

Few issues generate more volatile debate than assessment and the debate can become particularly intense when it concerns testing children in early childhood grades. Many early childhood educators contend that too much testing is done, too many erroneous decisions about young learners are made because of test data and too little credibility is afforded to classroom teachers as assessors of young children's learning (Meisels 1987; National Association of Early Childhood Specialists in State Departments of Education 1987; see also *Young Children*, 48, July 1993). Indeed, teachers seem to have been left out of the process of evaluating the students they teach (Pearson and Valencia 1987; Hills 1993), even though in many ways most early childhood teachers are very capable of stating how well and in what ways their students are learning. Through observations such as looking at a piece of student's writing and listening to students' reading, teachers can usually tell what students know and how to help them continue to grow.

The debate about early childhood testing ranges widely. Some critics argue that no testing should be done until children have been in school for at least three years, while others suggest that external measures and commercial tests can be relegated to their proper perspective by balancing the data they produce with information from teachers' own observations and from analysis of student work. This balance would underscore the necessity for assessment instruments and methodologies to be developmentally appropriate for and culturally-sensitive to the population with which they are to be used (Salinger 1996).

As criticisms of standardized, commercial tests have increased, many educators have come to recognize that assessment and testing are integral parts of a dynamic system that can dramatically influence what teachers teach, even if student evaluation depends primarily on external, standardized measures.

An example of this is the tendency of many teachers to 'teach to the test', thereby essentially letting test content determine curriculum (Shephard and Smith 1988).

Realization of the systemic effect of testing and assessment has played a central role in the impetus to move away from external commercial measures and toward 'alternative', 'authentic', 'performance-based', or 'portfolio' assessments in many content areas. These newer forms of assessment are designed to place teachers and children firmly in the centre of formal assessment, thereby affirming what many teachers have long found to be their most valuable kinds of data about learners.

One key to understanding the emphasis currently being placed on alternatives to standardized testing is understanding the distinction between testing and assessment (Chittenden 1991). Testing has traditionally involved using instruments with specific psychometric properties to gather data about children's performance on single, isolated occasions. These instruments, usually developed and scored by commercial testing companies or state agencies, are external to the schools where they are used. Assessment, on the other hand, implies an ongoing process that results in richer, potentially more useful, and varied information about students. While specific instruments or test-like tasks may be used, assessment methodologies are contextualized within the fabric of children's classrooms; activities mirror what students do every day. Their ultimate purpose is to present a cumulative portrait of learners' strengths, weaknesses and capabilities that will enable teachers to help each child learn more efficiently.

A district case study

Interest in performance assessment is widespread in the United States and many teachers have adopted alternative assessments for their own classroom use. As yet, relatively few school districts have actually undertaken the massive job of moving to systemic use of alternatives to standardized, multiple-choice testing, remaining instead at the exploratory stage, trying to determine how and if to proceed into this arena. However, one district in central New Jersey has made tremendous strides in reforming its assessment practices. The development and implementation of an early literacy portfolio in its early childhood programme has been the linchpin of change, motivating new assessment in upper grades and in mathematics instruction.

The portfolio has emerged slowly, the result of several years' work on the part of the district's teachers. In some ways, it is not unlike portfolio assessment approaches introduced into many schools in the last few years (Lamme and Hysmith 1991; Valencia, Hiebert and Afflerbach 1994); but this portfolio project differs from many such efforts in that its development has been grounded in particular research and theory. As in many districts, work on the portfolio was carried out by teams of teachers who invested emotionally and intellectually in the changes they sought to bring about. Here, however, teachers received support from their administrators, who provided time to think and plan and resources to implement their ideas.

The district is relatively typical of the Mid-Atlantic region of the United States. It is medium in size, with a student population of 4,500 that is ethnically and racially diverse; many children qualify for instruction in English as a second language. As New York City sprawl extends farther and farther from the city limits, the rural nature of the district has changed gradually to semirural and suburban. The district supports seven elementary schools, each of which has some degree of autonomy in its decision-making processes. The student population and teaching staff are relatively stable, and the teachers in the early childhood and elementary grades are mostly seasoned professionals.

The portfolio has been allowed to change over time but to change in a systematic way that reflects efforts to validate the portfolio and investigate its effectiveness as a replacement for a commercial, standardized test. The development phase spanned six years, although school administrators and teachers claim that the current version of the portfolio is, and will continue to be, 'in draft'. Figure 2.1 presents a chronology of the development of the portfolio system. The portfolio enjoys full district-wide implementation at the kindergarten, first- and second-grade levels. How the teachers and administrators developed and implemented the early literacy portfolio is described in this chapter.

Figure 2.1 Chronology: early literacy portfolio

School Year 1987–88:	Need for instructional change in the early childhood grades recognized at district level.
Sept. 88–June 89:	Study groups established and in-service opportunities provided for interested teachers; the study groups met after school and had access to a vast library of current books on early childhood teaching and learning. A new early childhood curriculum is developed and implemented.
Summer 1989:	'Lab school' established for teachers to build their understanding of new methodologies, including strategies such as story retellings that would be critical to the portfolio system. First draft of portfolio is developed in response to district challenge that

continued . . .

	if teachers wanted to discontinue use of a standardized test in first grade, they had to suggest an alternative.
Sept. 89–June 90:	Use of portfolio is initiated in small sample of kindergarten classes.
June 90:	Second draft of portfolio is developed with input from field test in small number of classes.
Summer 1990:	'Lab school' is provided for new teachers to learn curriculum and assessment methods.
Sept. 90–June 91:	Portfolio is used in all kindergarten classes.
Dec. 90–Feb. 91:	Drafts 1–3 of scale are developed, validated against students' portfolios, and refined.
June 91:	Scale is used by kindergarten teachers, with scores reported to district for accountability purposes.
July 91:	Fourth draft of portfolio is developed.
Sept. 91–June 92:	Use of portfolio in kindergarten and first grade classes extends assessment system. Portfolio procedures are 'standardized' based on teachers' suggestions and district's accountability needs; standardized test is eliminated.
Sept. 92–June 93:	All early childhood classes, kindergarten to grade two, use portfolio; at the end of the year, second graders who have kept portfolios since kindergarten take their collected work home to share with families. Additional drafts, 4 and 5, of the scale are developed.
Sept. 92 onward	Additional pieces such as the higher order thinking activity and a reading/writing checklist are added to accommodate teachers' perceived needs; draft 6 of the scale is developed.

Phase one: study and organizing for change

About ten years ago, the district's assistant superintendent for instruction focused her attention on the early childhood (kindergarten through grade two) curriculum and decided that change was needed. Instruction was traditional, full of activities designed to get children 'ready' for reading and 'give them language skills' to handle school work. Classrooms were extremely teacher-centred and instruction was skills-based. The administrator wanted to initiate a new orientation that would affirm the language skills, knowledge base and exploratory nature children bring with them at school entry. She envisioned teachers moving toward early childhood instruction that would be less didactic and more attuned to individuals' capabilities and needs.

Knowing that this kind of change will not take place unless teachers realigned their thinking about young learners, the administrator invited key teachers to form 'study groups' in which they would examine existing curriculum and investigate possibilities for change. Classroom release time allowed teachers to meet and a library of current books was provided for study and discussion. Additionally, outsiders, researchers from the nearby headquarters of the test development company, Educational Testing Service (ETS), were invited to act as 'critical friends' of the project. Their role was to ask questions, provide information and serve as a resource to the teachers; at no time did they intrude upon the process undertaken by the teachers themselves.

These two factors, formalized study groups and external critical 'friends', were important to the strong foundation upon which change has been built. In the study groups, teachers reflected upon their current practice and attitudes and identified areas they wanted to change. The literature available for their study provided new ideas and validated some of their own thinking about child development and instruction. The 'critical friends' at times offered alternate interpretations of what teachers read or thought, but mostly they affirmed the change process that was under way. Teachers read and talked about child development and literacy acquisition; they attended workshops, conferences, and university classes; they compared what they were discovering to what they did and said in their own class-rooms. The teachers were dealing with theories, accepting some, rejecting others, and in the process they developed their own theoretical stance about the education of young children.

While teachers' attention was directed toward the early childhood curriculum as a whole, the most significant changes at the classroom level seemed to be in literacy instruction:

- Teachers acknowledged that children knew tremendous amounts about reading and writing before school entry and sought ways to capitalize on that knowledge.
- After learning about invented spelling, they gave children logs in which to record their thoughts.
- After thinking about the discontinuity between good children's litera-ture and the basal reader series they had been using, they increased the size of their classroom libraries and phased out the basals.
- They discussed the valuable information that can be gained by closely observing children and developed observational sheets on which to record anecdotal and other notes.

Developing and refining their new approaches was very satisfying to many of the teachers; they felt themselves to be part of a collaborative effort that had benefits for them as professionals and for the children they taught.

Teachers were, however, dismayed when students' scores on the standardized test administered to first-graders were not skyrocketing as validation of curriculum changes. Concern that scores seemed at best static led teachers to analyse the content of the standardized test used by the district. They noticed the discontinuity between its subskill focus and the more holistic thrust of their 'emergent literacy' curriculum, and like many other teachers who have been involved in curriculum reform, they concluded that the standardized test was not providing a real measure of their students' achievement. Further, the teachers surmised that it was unlikely that any multiple choice test would ever measure their students' levels accurately. They also were beginning to realize that the source of valuable assessment data could be found within their own classrooms.

Teachers sought the support of their administration in suspending use of the commercial, standardized test, which was not mandated by the state. The administration has been characterized 'not only by its visionary dedication to teachers but also by its hard-headedness about evaluation' (Mitchell 1992: 160). It was not surprising, then, that the official response to the teachers' request was a challenge to develop an alternate form of assessment that could be used for accountability purposes and that would demonstrate adequate levels of reliability and validity.

Phase two: beginnings of the portfolio

Teachers' continuing study and discussion led them to conclude that they wanted to develop a portfolio to assess students' early literacy development. The primary purpose of their proposed portfolio would be to document children's literacy learning, that is, to provide for each child a descriptive record that is richer and more useful than test scores alone. Documentation as an alternative to traditional assessment is responsive to each child's capabilities and goes a long way toward ensuring that no child gets lost in the system (Chittenden and Courtney 1989). Using a portfolio approach to documentation makes it possible to demonstrate the many different ways young children can work toward mutually-agreed standards of competence.

In the assessment scheme devised in the teachers' study groups, the portfolio would stay with the students through the kindergarten, first and second grades, gradually growing in size to provide a longitudinal record of achievement in reading and writing. Work samples, 'test-like' records such as running records, teachers' observational notes, and miscellaneous other entries would provide the actual evidence of progress. Thus, the portfolio would not be a collection of 'best' works annotated by the students; it would instead be a teacher record-keeping process built around performance evidence from the classroom, which could be used outside the classroom as well.

From the district's perspective, the portfolio would have to be a valid measure of students' achievement in literacy. This criterion did not mean that portfolios would have to look identical in all classes in all seven elementary schools in the district but did mean that contents of students' portfolios would have to be comparable enough that teachers would be able to pick up the portfolios of their colleagues' students, children whom they do not know, and draw accurate conclusions about these learners' progress in reading and writing.

First efforts

The first draft of the portfolio was little more than a folder of teacher-developed observational checklists and other highly abbreviated indicators of students' growth in reading and writing. In many ways, the initial portfolio was designed for efficiency and for student comparisons. Teachers would fill out forms and include them in a portfolio, forsaking the richness of student work for the economy of checklists.

Teachers knew that their plan was just a beginning but they considered it good enough to merit pilot testing in several kindergarten classes. It is important that the teachers gave their ideas this period of limited use and review, rather than implementing the portfolio immediately in all kindergarten classes during the first year. At the end of pilot testing, teachers analysed results and realized that they needed finer-grained assessments, fewer checklists, and more students' work. When viewed in isolation from classroom dynamics, the checklists were a static form of assessment that retrospectively provided little insight into children's learning. The portfolio needed to be a bit 'messier', even if that meant rethinking what they needed to see from each student and how they would go about collecting evidence. Teachers had realized that they needed to draw upon what one of their 'critical friends', ETS developmental psychologist Edward Chittenden (1991), has called the 'database for literacy assessment'. This database, he says, is 'potentially a broad one indeed'.

As teachers incorporate greater variety of activities and materials into their reading programme, the base will become more solid. It is true that teachers worry that they won't know 'where the children are' when they shift from a single-dimension basal programme to a literature-based approach. But these same teachers will be in a position to know much more about the child as a reader – interests, choices, strategies, skills – because the opportunities for assessment have multiplied.

Enriching the portfolio contents

As they had done throughout the portfolio development process, teachers collaborated in their attempts to gather richer evidence about student performance. They decided to administer Clay's (1979) Concepts about Print (see also Clay 1985) test to students several times a year and to include writing samples and tallies of students' retelling of unfamiliar stories (Morrow 1988). In addition to the writing samples, teachers wanted a more direct measure of invented spelling and developed a 'Word Awareness Writing Activity', or WAWA, based on the work of Richard Gentry and others who have maintained that children's invented spelling offers insight into how they come to understand phonemic structure. Interviews with each child and with parents, a self-portrait and observational records to gather additional information rounded out the revised portfolio.

These basic components have remained the core of the portfolio, although over years of use additions have been made to gather information on students' comprehension and thinking skills and strategies. The chart in Figure 2.2 presents all entries that are currently included in the portfolio and shows the approximate times during the year when materials are collected. The chart is attached to each child's portfolio, a sturdy accordion-pleated folder. Many teachers collect samples more frequently than required and many allow students to put work samples into their portfolios if they wish.

Extending portfolio use

After the 'enriched' portfolio was used for a year in all kindergarten classes in the district, children's portfolios were included among the records passed along to students' first-grade teachers. Thus, the portfolio spread: kindergarten teachers began anew with their in-coming students; first-graders added more to their portfolios, and then into the second grade. Thus, there was a gradual system-wide implementation of the new assessment system, with ample time for fine tuning of procedures and contents as need arose.

At the end of the first full year of kindergarten implementation, teachers met in small groups to discuss the year-long portfolios. Teachers brought portfolios for several children, one doing well, one experiencing difficulty, and one whose performance was puzzling or ambiguous. In preparation, teachers analysed these portfolios thoroughly so they could ground their comments in the actual evidence contained in the portfolios, rather than in their knowledge of the children in a classroom setting. At the meeting, teachers exchanged portfolios and, working in pairs, they went about the task of interpreting the work of each other's students. The pairs of teachers discussed the students whose work they had studied, referencing their conclusions about performance to the portfolio contents.

Figure 2.2 Graphic showing schedule for collection of portfolio entries. This graphic is attached to each child's portfolio as a record-keeping device; it shows times during each school year when specific entries are collected for inclusion in the portfolios.

SOUTH BRUNSWICK BOARD OF EDUCATION

Student's Name _____ School _____

Teacher's Name _____ Date of Entrance _____

	Pre K	Beg K	Mid K	End K	Beg 1	Mid 1	End 1	Beg 2	Mid 2	End 2
1 Self Portraits	*	*		*	*		*	*		*
2 Interviewing with Child		*			*			*		
3 Interview with the Parent	*	*			*			*		
4 Concept about Print Test		*		*						
5 Word Awareness Writing Activity (WAWA)			*	*	*	*	*		*	*
6 Sight Word List				*	*	*	*		*	*
7 Reading Sample				*	*	*		*	*	*
8 Writing Sample		*		*	*	*	*	*	*	*
9 Class Record			*			*			*	
10 Story Retelling	*	*	*	*	*	*	*	*	*	*
11 Optional Forms										
12 Higher Order Comprehension								*	*	*

* Asterisk indicates approximate time to enter an item in the portfolio. Teachers are expected to enter items when they need the data. Items should reflect current levels of literacy.

Teachers were genuinely surprised at how accurately they could evaluate information about students whom they did not know merely by looking at the collected work samples. In many ways, this realization was the most important step forward in developing the early literacy portfolio, for here was the paradigm shift that encouraged teachers to move toward confidence in their ability to make judgements about students' overall performance on the basis of the collected work samples. Teachers saw the transfer value of the portfolio contents and agreed to send work samples as well as summary information forward to the next year's teachers.

Phase three: 'standardizing' the portfolio

As indicated on the chart in Figure 2.1, student work is collected at several designated times each year. The actual compilation of work for a portfolio and its analysis take place at intervals roughly coinciding with parent conferences and district-mandated reporting of student progress. Teachers use many strategies to collect student evidence, compile portfolios and evaluate them (Salinger and Chittenden 1994). Most teachers keep work folders from which they and the students can select writing samples to supplement the running records and other documents that the teachers have been collecting. Some teachers photocopy journal entries that seem to be especially good indicators of student growth. Many teachers collect work more frequently than required, especially for students who seem to be experiencing difficulty. Because the portfolio is used for accountability purposes teachers must be certain to include all documents necessary to give a thorough picture of each student. Still, many teachers allow considerable student selection of work to supplement the basic, required pieces.

The emergent literacy scale

A critical issue confronting the teachers who developed the portfolio was its credibility and use beyond their classrooms. In an abstract sense, the question was whether a assessment system aligned with instruction could be used to inform the policy decisions of administrators and school boards, and communicate adequately to parents. In a pragmatic sense, the teachers wanted the portfolio to be used for accountability because they wanted to be rid of the first-grade standardized test. These issues reflect the tension between the teachers' and students' needs for data elaboration and the district's needs for data reduction and summary and for comparisons of students.

- How could rich, qualitative evidence of observational records and students' work samples be summarized to meet district accountability needs without trivializing, or distorting, the data or diminishing their value for making classroom decisions?
- Could the data be used effectively on two distinctly different levels?

The answers seemed to lie in being able to assign to the portfolio some kind of score that would have enough psychometric rigour to serve the district's purpose. Thus, teachers and 'critical friends' undertook the task of designing the scale of early literacy development that would become the core of the portfolio system. Together, they studied many existing scales used to describe what young children do and how their products and academic performance look at various stages of emergent literacy. Dissatisfied with the scales they reviewed, they began to develop their own scale by referring to evidence collected in many student portfolios and writing detailed behavioural descriptors of levels that span development from a level typical of most children at kindergarten entry through typical achievement at the completion of second grade. Their goal was to provide a robust enough picture of how students 'look' and perform as they move from preliteracy to more competent stages of ability that it could be used as a metric for summarizing children's growth at several distinct levels.

It is important to note, however, that the scale draws attention to only one aspect of early literacy, those strategies children possess for making sense of and with print; it does not reflect the breadth of children's interests in literacy, nor of their understanding except as reflected in the quality of their writing and their retellings.

Even in its first iterations, the six-point scale was a developmental instrument referenced directly to contemporary research and practice, not a conventional scoring rubric like those used to evaluate writing. Descriptors were written for each point on the scale. Each point represents a phase in development of children's abilities to make sense of and with print, and the language used for each point expresses a developmental continuum. The scale can be described as theory referenced because its interpretation is linked to an understanding of the processes of literacy acquisition. The scale can also be described as grounded in practice because evidence of students' progress along the continuum can be found in work samples and observational records contained in the portfolios. In many ways, teachers' thinking as they developed the scale can be traced to much of the reading they had done as they modified and fine-tuned their literacy curriculum.

After trying to use their first draft of the scale to rank students' portfolios, teachers fine-tuned their descriptors by making language richer and more evocative of the developmental phases of emergent literacy. The process of honing their language for precision led teachers to add pieces to the portfolio, as they realized that some aspects of development were not fully captured by the existing contents. Finally, after four drafts, teachers found that their 'anchors' or descriptions of each level were indeed clear enough to demonstrate alignment with what students actually did as they progressed toward literacy. Independent of each other, two or more teachers could look at the same students' portfolios, compare the work to the scale, and place the students on the scale with high degrees of agreement The teachers have subsequently gone on to develop two additional drafts; aspects of the sixth draft are highlighted in Figure 2.3.

Figure 2.3 Highlights of the six-point early literacy scale

LEVELS

6 Advanced independent reader
- Uses multiple strategies flexibly
- Monitors and self-corrects literacy behaviours
- Controls most conventions of writing and spelling

5 Early independent reader
- Handles familiar material on own but needs some support with unfamiliar material
- Draws on multiple cues to figure out unfamiliar words and self-correct
- Uses strategies such as rereading and guessing
- Has large, stable sight vocabulary
- Understands conventions of writing

4 Advanced beginning reader
- Uses major cueing system for word identification and self-correction
- Requires some support with unfamiliar materials
- Shows awareness of letter patterns and conventions of writing, such as full stops and capitalization

3 Early beginning reader
- Shows sense of letter-sound correspondence and concept of word
- Uses syntax and story line to predict unfamiliar words in new material
- Has small but stable sight vocabulary
- Shows awareness of beginning and ending sounds in invented spelling

2 Advanced emergent reader
- Engages in pretend reading and writing
- Uses sense of story structure, predictable language, and picture cues in retelling stories; retellings use approximations of booklike language
- Can anticipate story elements
- Attempts to use letters in writing

1 Early emergent reader
- Shows awareness of some conventions of book structure (such as back and front) and the distinction between pictures and text
- Shows little understanding that print conveys meaning in books and other documents; thinks meaning is external to print
- Shows little interest in reading for himself or herself; although is interested in listening to stories
- Notices some environmental print

Teachers who developed this scale would advise colleagues who want to use such a means to evaluate their own students' work to discuss the terms used as labels and the behavioural descriptors for the six points in order to develop their own ways of thinking and talking about these aspects of emergent literacy. Also note that the behaviours suggested under each of the six points is only a sampling of the behaviours listed by the teachers who developed the scale.

Using the scale

At the middle and end of each school year, teachers evaluate the contents of their students' portfolios and provide a judgement about each student's point on the scale to the district. The ratings are used to monitor general student progress and to meet state and local evaluation requirements. For example, the portfolio scores have replaced a standardized test as part of the evidence used when referring children to federally funded programmes such as Title I or other special services.

To ensure the reliability of teachers' ratings, all kindergarten, first- and second-grade teachers submit a sample of their students' scored portfolios to be used during yearly moderation (calibration) meetings that are held in January or February. In addition to verifying the accuracy of teachers' use of the scale, these sessions provide an overview of the scale and training on its use to teachers new to the district. During the meetings, teachers' sample portfolios receive a second, blind reading by teachers who come to know the children only through studying evidence in the portfolios and assigning a second score. Interrater reliability, calculated each year, has been consistently high (90s), an indication to the district that the portfolios produce sound, meaningful assessment data (Bridgeman, Chittenden, and Cline, 1995; Salinger and Chittenden, 1994).

While these high interrater reliability coefficients are reassuring, the real value of the sessions seems to reside in the moderation process itself. Without a doubt, the selection of one's own students' work samples and use of the scale call for complex levels of judgement and decision-making by individual teachers. Still, the moderation meetings, during which teachers review the documents in unfamiliar students' portfolios and discuss interpretations with colleagues, promote a common understanding about the assessment of early literacy and a shared appreciation of the district's early childhood curriculum. The benefits of this assessment system can thus be seen to accrue as much from the teachers' increased professional engagement and sense of themselves as competent professionals as from their use of the portfolio in their own classrooms.

Assessing the assessment

After three years of implementing the literacy portfolio in all the early childhood classes of the district, it seemed appropriate to gather some information about its use. One aspect of this investigation involved interviewing teachers who had used the portfolio to gather their impressions about its effectiveness and their ideas for improving its use. Sixty-three teachers responded to questions in an interview that took thirty to forty-five minutes. Responses were coded and analysed by three independent researchers.

How the teachers accommodated the management aspects of the portfolio was of particular interest. No matter what mechanism teachers devised to store student work, they all commented on the sheer quantity of paper generated by the assessment system and their difficulties storing the documentation with some degree of security and confidentiality. There were many different strategies for collecting student work and conducting the one-on-one interchanges required for the running records and story retelling components, e.g. keeping two folders, one for the student work, the other for observational notes, recording sheets from running records and retellings, and any other records that had to be kept secure. The student work included original writing, photocopies of journal pages that seemed especially important, records of books read, and any other work that either the teacher or the students themselves thought worthy of saving for assessment use.

Teachers also developed numerous means for finding time to conduct one-on-one conferences with students. Collecting story retellings posed particular challenges for the obvious reason that very little time should elapse between when students hear or read a story and their opportunity to provide a retelling to the teacher. Teachers often read to a story to small group of students and then collected individual story retellings from participants as quickly as possible, hoping that each retelling would be speedy so that children would still remember what they had heard when their turns came. Often children were encouraged to fold paper into thirds and draw pictures of the beginning, middle and end of the stories they heard; these drawings provided memory support for their turn with the teacher. Even with such elaborate schemes, teachers often could not hear every child at the first attempt and would have to include children in another listening group.

Collecting retellings became somewhat easier as children gained more skills. Teachers encouraged listeners to draw and write brief notes which could again be the guides for retellings. These written commentaries provided additional documentation to support the actual retelling checklist. As more and more children could actually read stories themselves and write more extended summaries, teachers were able to schedule retellings more efficiently. By second grade many children turned in written retellings for their portfolios, as an alternative, and these were evaluated using criteria similar to those used for oral retellings.

Collecting running records provided equal challenges. Teachers kept a small library of books separate from the class library and used these unfamiliar books for this aspect of the assessment. Finding time to spend with each child demanded that teachers plan periods when children were working independently or with peers on projects that they could complete without direct supervision or instruction.

About half of the teachers maintained that management did not represent a major issue in their classrooms because they had woven the portfolio activities into their classroom routines. Many suggested that on the whole the assessment procedures blended well with everyday practice and that management issues were minor in comparison to the value of the assessment system. For example, collecting writing samples, listening to children read, or asking them about sight words, were a part of ongoing instruction; periodically documenting these activities for the portfolio was relatively easy. One teacher said that she didn't find the 'portfolio much work – it just kind of happens [because] it's just what you're doing anyway'. She stated that she 'integrates the portfolio collection into daily routines [and] makes copies of many pieces' that she thinks might be good documentation for the portfolio. Most of the positive comments stressed the value of the portfolio for the teachers themselves, but one teacher said, 'It's a very nonthreatening way to test a kid'.

A possible explanation for the teachers' positive sentiment is the order in which change had occurred in these early childhood classrooms, curriculum change first followed by development and implementation of the portfolio. The teachers had become accustomed to their child-centred curriculum; they could navigate comfortably around its procedures and could readily see that the portfolio was indeed a logical part of what they themselves had developed in the name of instructional reform.

Of course, it is important to note that for about one third of the teachers, the issue of management and time was of major concern; but even these teachers said that they considered the assessment worth the effort. One said, 'It's difficult to find the time. Sometimes I stop teaching and send kids to work in the centres'. She, like others, felt that assessment sometimes competed with teaching. Another, relatively new to teaching, noted, 'Time is really a problem, but you get better at it. Training is extremely important. I think it becomes more manageable as you have better understanding'.

Many teachers noted the importance of training and staff development, provided early in the school year and focused on procedures and underlying theory. Recommendations applied to new teachers, to those new to the portfolio system and to those who merely want to upgrade their skills. One teacher stressed the importance of sharing with colleagues those procedures that seemed to work well in managing the system. Such comments are further testament to the curriculum change and portfolio development as important vehicles for bringing about a cohesive professional community among the district early childhood teachers.

Conclusions

In this district, teachers worked together to align their instruction and assessment and in so doing, they came to feel confident in their abilities to make sound instructional decisions and to communicate meaningfully with parents. Their efforts showed thoughtful planning, careful field testing, willingness to revise and change direction, and collegial interactions among peers and with administrators and external 'critical friends'. The development of the portfolio was clearly a significant undertaking on the part of the teachers, one worth their time and energies.

Yet, by its very nature, any classroom-based assessment system must remain dynamic, just as teaching and learning are dynamic forces. Teachers, administrators, policy-makers and parents are justified in wanting an assessment system that is stabilized, mutually understood and easily interpreted, but any classroom-based assessment system must remain open to improvement and responsive to classroom needs. This tension between stability and responsiveness suggests that to be truly useful, any portfolio and its components must continually be reviewed and evaluated by all who have a stake in its efficacy and usefulness. Without this constant review and adjustment, any assessment system can become static and routine, merely a set of procedures to be completed, much like the externally-imposed standardized tests it is supposed to replace. In the words of one of the veteran teachers in the district, the biggest mistake that can be made is 'assuming that the portfolio system is in place – it must be kept "in process" or it will not be used much or used enthusiastically'.

References

Bridgeman, B., Chittenden, E. and Cline, F. (1995) *Characteristics of a Portfolio Scale for Rating Early Literacy*, Princeton, NJ: Center for Performance Assessment of Educational Testing Service.

Chittenden, E. (1991) 'Authentic assessment, evaluation, and documentation of student performance', in V. Perrone (ed.) *Expanding Student Assessment* (pp. 22–31), Alexandria, VA: Association for Supervision and Curriculum Development.

Chittenden, E. and Courtney, R. (1989) 'Assessment of young children's reading: documentation as an alternative to testing', in D.S. Strickland and L.M. Morrow (eds.) *Emerging Literacy: Young Children Learn to Read and Write* (pp. 107–20), Newark, DE: International Reading Association.

Clay, M.M. (1979) *Reading: The Patterning of Complex Behaviour,* Portsmouth, NH: Heinemann.

—— (1985) *The Early Detection of Reading Difficulties,* 3rd edn, Auckland, NZ: Heinemann.

Gomez, M.L., Graue, M.E. and Bloch, M.N. (1991) 'Reassessing portfolio assessment: rhetoric and reality', *Language Arts* 68: 620–8.

Hills, T. (1993) 'Assessment in context: teachers and children at work', *Young Children* 48: 20–8.

Lamme, L.L. and Hysmith, C. (1991) 'One school's adventure into portfolio assessment', *Language Arts* 68: 629–40.

Meisels, S.J. (1987) 'Uses and abuses of developmental screening and school readiness testing', *Young Children* 42(2): 4–9, 68–73.

Mitchell, R. (1992) *Testing for Learning: How New Approaches to Evaluation Can Improve American Schools*, New York: Free Press.

Morrow, L. M. (1988) 'Retelling stories as a diagnostic tool', in S.M. Glazer, L.W. Searfoss, L. Gentile (eds) *Reexamining Reading Diagnosis: New Trends and Procedures* (pp. 128–49), Newark, DE: International Reading Association.

National Association of Early Childhood Specialists in State Departments of Education. (1987). *Unacceptable Trends in Kindergarten Entry and Placement: A Position Statement,* Chicago: Author.

Pearson, P.D. and Valencia, S.W. (1987). 'Assessment, accountability, and professional prerogative', in J.E. Readence and R.S. Baldwin (eds) *Research in Literacy: Merging Perspectives* (pp. 3–16), Rochester, NY: National Reading Conference.

Salinger, T. and Chittenden, E. (1994) 'Analysis of an early literacy portfolio: Consequences for instruction', *Language Arts* 71: 446–52.

Salinger, T. (1996). *Literacy for Young Children,* Columbus, OH: Merrill/Prentice Hall.

Shephard, L.A. and Smith, M.L. (1988) 'Flunking kindergarten: escalating curriculum leaves many behind', *American Educator* 12(2): 34–8.

South Brunswick Board of Education (1992) *Early Childhood Education: A Guide For Parents and Children,* South Brunswick, NJ: Author.

Valencia, S.W., Hiebert, E.H. and Afflerbach, P.P. (1994) *Authentic Reading Assessment: Practices and Possibilities*, Newark, DE: International Reading Association.

3

TAKING A CLOSER LOOK AT READING

A Scottish Perspective

Louise Hayward and Ernie Spencer

There can be few more terrifying experiences for any teacher than realizing for the first time that you are responsible for developing and enhancing children's abilities in reading. It seems such a complex area and one in which it always appears that others know so much more than you do; at times it can feel like facing the dragon from children's literature. Classrooms can still be lonely places, for not all teachers have the opportunity to work collaboratively and what we learn about reading as teachers is still often a matter of chance. Sometimes everything depends on whether we work in a school where other teachers have been thinking about reading, whether courses are on offer in our area, whether or not we are able to attend. Yet there is nothing more satisfying than watching children's reading develop, watching their pleasure as, with increasing confidence, they encounter more complex texts and more complex tasks. But how can we have confidence that the advice we offer to children about their reading is sound? How can we be sure that the action we propose to take to enhance children's reading is informed?

'Taking a Closer Look at Reading' is a package of diagnostic procedures which has been designed to address some of these very real concerns. The project which led to the production of this package involved teachers, policy-makers and researchers, working together to integrate their respective knowledge and experience. Their aim was to develop a resource for teachers which would provide practical, research-based advice on strategies which, as far as we can tell from present knowledge, are most likely to be effective in helping children to become confident and competent readers able to perceive and pursue meaning in what they read. This chapter describes five case studies of teachers using the procedures in practice with children who have differing reading abilities. The case studies illustrate how the procedures can be built into everyday classroom activities in a wide range of reading contexts. They also demonstrate that the approaches advocated are the same for all learners – identify what the child can do and build from there, recognize strengths, encourage confidence and provide practical ideas as to how progress might be made.

Our work in classrooms confirmed what we already believed: the professionalism of the teacher and the right kind of relationship between teacher and child are vital for success. So it was crucial to propose procedures which *supported* teachers' professionalism. Our material does not provide 'expert diagnostic instruments' to substitute for the teacher's professional judgement. Rather, they offer a framework of ideas intended to help the teacher to assess strengths and needs and consider next steps for herself or himself. Many of the ideas in the package will be familiar, highlighting the fact that there is already a great deal of effective practice in schools. 'Taking a Closer Look at Reading' should confirm and extend this good practice. It should help to build our confidence as teachers that the advice we offer to support children's reading and the action we propose are informed both by research and by good practice. The package has, we hope, the potential to make our learning experiences as teachers less subject to chance.

'Taking a Closer Look at Reading': the package

In keeping with the view that assessment should be set firmly in the context of learning and teaching, 'Taking a Closer Look at Reading' emphasizes from the start the purpose/s for which reading is undertaken.

A key theme is the idea that the pupils themselves should have an important role in determining what to read and for what purposes. They should also be actively involved, usually with the teacher, perhaps sometimes with other pupils, in describing and thinking about their own ways of reading. For the teacher, knowing what children think is crucial for good decisions about what to do next and involving them in the decision-making is likely to encourage their commitment to any proposed action. The package moves on from these important general points to introduce the four areas for exploration which form the framework of the procedures. In any reading task, pupils try to make sense of what is on the page – search for meaning – in terms of their own experience. The research tells us that effective readers fix on and recognize every word as they scan the text at speed. There are also indications that they also often use their knowledge and experience and the context of the particular text to make predictions about the continuation of a sentence, chapter, theme or plot. This process of predicting and searching for meaning can result in effective reading but it can also interfere with understanding if readers make the wrong 'guesses'. The four areas for exploration are intended to help teachers to help pupils deal with both key processes – recognize words and sentences and use their own experience of life effectively to construct sense:

- attitude and motivation may be important for reading in general or for a particular task;
- decoding deals with the ways in which pupils may recognize words and sentences;
- pursuit of meaning considers issues related to the pupils' use of prior experience and all the context cues within the text to construct their own perceptions of what the text is about;
- awareness of the author's use of language offers ideas about how pupils learn about the author's choice of words, images and structures to convey meaning, stimulate the readers' imagination and achieve effects.

While in reality these four aspects of the reading process are interrelated, in practice as teachers we have to work with pupils to prioritize next steps in learning. In this context it may be useful to think of the four areas separately to help us analyse children's work, recognize areas of strength and identify appropriate next steps. This approach which identifies strengths, areas for exploration and possible next steps is one which is appropriate for all readers, from the beginning reader to the most competent. The procedures are intended to be used to support all learners and are not focused on the needs of any particular group.

In our work in schools, a number of teachers suggested that, although as teachers we are aware of the impact of such factors as attitude and motivation on reading, in practice our actions to support children's reading tend to focus on the mechanics of the reading process, e.g. on decoding. Putting ideas into practice is much more challenging than being aware of them. The case studies which follow show how the procedures have been interpreted by different teachers in practice in a range of different contexts, in primary and in secondary schools. They show teachers working with readers who are at an early stage of development and with others whose skills in reading are more sophisticated. In each instance the crucial issue is to identify what the child can do and to build from there. The examples we have chosen all focus on individual children but the issues which they exemplify are common and it would often be perfectly possible to apply the next steps described to small groups of readers.

Case Study One

Evidence from observation and discussion

'I can't read and I would really like to be able to.'

Lynne was 7 years old when she confided in her teacher. Her teacher was really concerned by the remark and determined to explore Lynne's reading with the learning support coordinator in the school. Why was reading such a challenge for Lynne and, more importantly, what might be done to help Lynne to achieve her aim?

Together the class teacher and the learning support teacher took a closer look at Lynne's reading. She had recently arrived from another school and her records showed that her teachers there had been extremely worried about her lack of progress in reading. In class Lynne was working on a different reading scheme from most of her classmates, since a miscue analysis had shown her reading book to be too difficult. As they observed her work in class both teachers noted Lynne's enthusiasm for tasks which were well within her capabilities: 'She was keen to show us what she had done. She needed constant praise. Her work was very neat and tidy and she took a lot of time over it. Lynne was taking a real interest in her reading books.'

Aware of the importance of exploring the learner's thinking and involving her in the decisions taken, the teachers determined to find out what Lynne thought about reading. After their discussion Lynne's class teacher believed that 'This was probably the most revealing of all the evidence gathered so far'. Lynne's concept of reading was very interesting. She enjoyed reading books from reading schemes and did not value library books. They were not as important as 'reading books': 'Mrs Smith has the reading books. The other teacher gives us library books. They're not reading books!' The appearance of the book mattered: 'I like books with nice pictures. I don't like books that've been scribbled on.'

Lynne did not find reading easy and was very much aware that she was not as good at it as some other children in her class. For this reason she preferred to read quietly to herself so that no-one could hear her mistakes: 'I like to read it into myself and not out loud because people will say – "Ah you can't read".' Even though she was having difficulties, Lynne thought that it was important that she learned to read. She had a very stereotypical vision of her future. She did realize that you would have to be able to read if you wanted a job, for example, as a teacher. However, her main aim was to become a mother: 'If you have a new born baby you can read to it and not make mistakes. I want to be a mother when I grow up.' She did not really appreciate that reading could be enjoyable or that you could learn from it beyond 'You wouldn't know what was on the telly if you couldn't read'.

Areas for exploration and possible next steps

As they considered the evidence before them, Lynne's teachers recognized that Lynne was coping well with her present reading scheme books but that there were a number of possible areas for development, if Lynne's reading abilities were to be enhanced. Initially they decided to focus on attitude and motivation, concentrating on strategies to build Lynne's confidence as a reader and to encourage a wider enjoyment of reading. Taking account of their knowledge of Lynne, the teachers decided on the next steps from 'Taking a Closer Look'.

CONFIDENCE

- Build in opportunities for Lynne to read to younger children.
- Ask Lynne to list all the things to do with reading at which she is 'good' and provide a record of achievement for her reading.

ENJOYMENT

- Introduce books beyond the reading scheme and encourage her enjoyment of it by asking her to recommend books for younger children.
- Build in rewards for undertaking tasks, e.g. taping her favourite story and allowing her group to listen to the tape.

As she reflected on working with Lynne, Lynne's teacher commented: 'I realized that reading in my classroom had been too scheme-based. Reading for Lynne meant books from the reading scheme. There are things about my teaching programme that I will look at again.'

Case Study Two

Evidence from a reading scheme

'You count the spaces and you fill in the words.'

Colin was 9 years old. He was quite clear about the fact that he did not like reading, but his teacher was delighted by his recent enthusiasm for *Fuzzbuzz* stories. He was on his eleventh story and had consistently been working very hard in class. Recently there had been a major breakthrough: he had been taking reading books home.

Colin's task was to read aloud one of the pages he had worked on at home and then to complete the sentences. The italicized words and other markings on the text show how Colin actually read it aloud. The text was accompanied by a cartoon of Big Don and Little Don in tammies and tartan, showing Big Don bumping Little Don with his elbow. Non-Scottish readers may not be familiar with 'croft', which is a small Highland farm.

Reading aloud:
Line

1 Big-Ben-does-not-see-little-things. /

    (tips)

2 He-*trips*-up-on them. /

    (tips)

3. He-*trips*-up-on-things-in-the-hills. /

    (tips)

4 He-*trips*-up-on-things-in-the-glen. /

    (tips)

5 He-*trips*-up-on-things-in-his-croft. /

    (tips)

6 He-does-not-*trip*-up-on-big-things. /

  B

7 *b*ecause-he-can-see-them. /

    (tips)

8 But-he-does-*trip*-up-on-little-things. /

    (tips)

9 In-the-end-he-*trips*-up-on-little-Don. /

    - = short pause

    / = longer pause

To provide a quick check on Colin's understanding his teacher asked him to complete a number of sentences using the words provided. This exercise is set out here in exactly the form in which Colin saw it, with his answers written in.

NB: It is crucial to place 'things' on the next line, as in the teachers' worksheet (because this led to Colin's error).

Words: *little*   *trips*   *croft*   *Don*

1 Big Ben does not see *Don*
things.

2 He *tips* up on them.

3 He trips up on things in his *croft*.

4 In the end he trips up on *little*.

As she listened to Colin his teacher noted that he read with enthusiasm one word at a time and took a big breath at the end of every sentence/ line. He began line 7 as if beginning a new sentence. He recognized all the words but consistently read 'tips' instead of 'trips'. He completed the sentences very quickly, getting two of them correct. But what did this evidence suggest? How much did Colin understand? Was this text too difficult for him? His teacher decided to investigate further.

A brief discussion with Colin about the follow-up task and how he had approached it proved to be illuminating.

Teacher: Can you tell me how to do this?
Colin: Well, you put the words at the top of the page into the spaces.
Teacher: How do you know which ones to put in which spaces?
Colin: It's about the story.
Teacher: How did you decide which word to put in which space?
Colin: It was easy. You read the story and get the answers . . . so . . . Big Ben does not see Don. He tips up on them. He tips up on things in his croft. And you have to use all the words so the last one is *little*.

Clearly there was no misunderstanding . . . but there were areas of Colin's reading which should be built upon. The teacher's view was:

> I would not concentrate on attitude and motivation with Colin. He enjoys *Fuzzbuzz* and is working hard. To begin with I would concentrate on decoding.
>
> In decoding I think there are two questions to consider. The first is, does Colin recognize the word 'trip' and does he know what it means? It was interesting that he made the same mistake when reading and when he completed the sentence. He wrote 'tips' and not 'trips'. I shall need to talk to him about that. I think that the most important 'next step' for Colin just now is about punctuation when reading. He reads lines as if they were sentences. If you look at his first answer – Don – it's right if you don't notice the word 'things' on the next line. Colin and Peter work well together. We talked about sentences and now they are taking turns to read sentences from their reading book.
>
> One other thing, I will add in more words to choose from in future, so that he can't just put the last word into the last space without reading it!
>
> I also think it is important to help Colin be a more fluent reader . . . perhaps paired reading might help.

Case Study Three

Evidence from non-fiction texts

'I do not believe in witchcraft.'

Lisa, aged 13, enjoyed English and had worked hard on the 'Witch Poems and Stories' unit devised by her teacher. She read a great deal of fiction but, when asked to undertake any research work, had simply until now copied out sections of text.

At this point in the unit Lisa was to undertake a piece of research and to present findings in the form of a written report. The focus of the research could be either *a*) Witchcraft – what is it? or *b*) Witches from the past. Lisa undertook the task with enthusiasm and produced the following report

Library Research

Witches are people who are supposed to worship a non-Christian god and to be able to cast magic spells for good or evil. They are said to fly at night on a wooden broom. There are lots of different tales about witches. In lots of different films and storys all the witches look the same, ugly face very old and always a black cloke. Lots of people believe that you became a witch by working with the devil. It is said that the witches are given there powers by the devil. Lots of books where writen about witches and all thier evil powers long ago. The people of the church thought that witch's should be caught and hanged. Between 1500 and 1750 200,000 people were killed because people thought that they were witches. I do not believe in witchcraft.

The teacher's reaction to Lisa's report was as follows:

Lisa has done some background reading for this report and has tried to use her own words rather than simply copying out chunks of text. She has presented a number of points of information, some of which are taken from reading, e.g. 'witches are people who are supposed to worship a non-Christian God' and 'between 1500 and 1750, 200,000 men and women were killed because people thought that they were witches'. However, I suspect that some ideas from her own experience came in: 'all witches look the same, ugly face very old and always a black cloke.' Her report is not really very well focused either on topic (*a*) or (*b*) but includes elements of both.

There is a sense of life about the response and interest in the subject which I would wish to maintain. We talked about her work and agreed to concentrate on Pursuit of Meaning. We decided to begin by separating out Lisa's ideas from ideas from library research (I was thinking of the exploration question in Taking a Closer Look, 'Do the pupils bring in their own ideas?') and to make the difference clear in the report. We also talked about different reading strategies ('Do pupils use a range of strategies appropriate to the purpose of reading?'). It became clear that Lisa always simply reads through text from beginning to end. Lisa is now going to work on incorporating skimming and scanning into her range of approaches to reading. She is working on this with one of her friends: they read pieces of text quickly and tell one another about the main ideas.

Case Study Four

Evidence from a class novel

John, aged 12, had always found reading difficult. Recent English work in his class had been based on 'A Pair of Jesus Boots' by Sylvia Sherry. The novel was more difficult reading than would be attempted by John in his own private choice of text. Over a period of time, sections of the novel were read aloud to a group of children by the teacher while John and a few others followed in their own copies of the text. Now and again, the teacher stopped to ask questions and invite discussion from the group. John participated well throughout.

The purpose of the task which John's group undertook was to develop the ability to follow certain threads or themes through a lengthy text. Thus, although particular episodes and passages received close attention, all discussion and writing related to the main theme – the development of the central character, Rocky O'Rourke.

John's task was to write about Rocky O'Rourke and to show how Rocky changed as the story developed.

A pair of Jesus boots and the author is Sylvia Sherry.
Rocky had a wee step sister and a big brother who was in jail for the first few chapters. Rocky wanted to be a criminal he lived in St. Cathrins Sqre. He is the leader of the cats. The cats were Chan, Bedeey, Nabber and Billy. They were boys that hung about shops and broke into shope. The cats did not like the chikes lot the cats like to fight with the chikes lot but chikes Joey was set up and went to jail and he was Rocky's hero and Joey got let out erly and when he got home he stole his mums money and went

a way and he wanted out of Liverpool because he was scard of Jim Sipson.

Rockys dad died and his mum got married with and other man who had a wee garl. Mr. Olaver was the man that looked after the flats and Rocky was playing football and he found out that he was a ex Liverpool player.

He chaneged when Joye got out of jail he did not like him for takeing the money from his mum so he did not want to be a criminal.

The teacher's reaction to John's work was as follows:

John has enjoyed 'Jesus Boots' and sometimes when we were reading the book talked to me about what he thought would happen next. His piece of writing shows that he has picked up a lot of information from the novel. He knew the Cats were Chan, Beady, Nabber and Billy and he has been able to make inferences about characters, such as 'Rocky wanted to be a criminal'.

He does show an awareness of the change in Rocky: 'Joey was set up and went to jail and he was Rocky's hero' and 'he (Rocky) did not like him for taking the money from his mum so he did not want to be a criminal'. There is an attempt to explain the change in Rocky by referring to his disillusion with his brother, Joey, when he witnesses Joey stealing from his mother.

There is evidence that John knows of other conflicting influences on Rocky (paragraph 3), but these are not linked explicitly to the change in Rocky. I would want to look at Pursuit of Meaning – at the questions on main points and following a line of argument. Perhaps it would help to give John's group a number of statements about Rocky and ask them to identify which of these were main ideas; or it might be useful to give the group a range of statements, some true, some not and ask John's group to choose which ones are true and to prove it from the text.

Case Study Five

Using evidence from across the curriculum

From observation of and discussion with Kerry it was clear to her teacher that Kerry's confidence as a reader is developing fast, after a period of slow progress. The shift in motivation seems to be related to a change in the reading scheme she was following to one she found easier to cope with.

In connection with their environmental studies topic, Kerry's class had been learning how to find information in reference books using the index and how to summarize the important points. They had been using an approach to the latter which involves three stages –

1   underlining key words in the text after reading it,
2   noting these in a separate page,
3   writing an account of the information they have obtained.

In the case of Kerry's group the teacher asked the pupils to underline words only on the first of the two pages (other groups did this for the whole text) and the teacher gave the group direct support and encouragement as they 'made the notes', transferring the underlined words to the separate page.

Surviving in the Desert

To make tents, <u>camel or goat hair</u> is collected by combing the animals. It is then <u>woven</u> into long strips which are sewn together. In the <u>Sahara, sheep's</u> wool is used. When wet, it expands and so keeps rain out. The largest piece is used for the tent roof. The side walls and the back can be <u>rolled up</u> to allow cool breezes to blow through it.

The tent is <u>low lying</u> to prevent winds and sandstorms from blowing it over. Although it is possible to stand up inside, people tend to <u>sit down</u> to avoid smoke from the fire. A wealthy sheikh may have a tent with four or five central <u>poles</u> instead of the <u>two or three</u> which are used to support smaller tents. The poles can be raised or lowered depending on the strength of the wind. Smaller poles are used to support the front, the back and the sides.

A curtain inside the tent divides the space into the male and female areas. The male section is the more public area; it has a fire around which people can sit and where coffee is made. Camel saddles and cushions are used as seating. The female area is used for storing spare clothes, sacks of grain, dates, coffee beans, and leather bags containing water and cooking utensils. There may also be a paraffin lamp, a radio and perhaps a sewing-machine.

Whether tent strips are bought or made, repairs need to be carried out and the whole tent may have to be taken apart each year to allow damaged strips to be replaced. There may be only a few tents in a camp or as many as thirty. These family groups move off together every week or two, when they need to find fresh grazing areas. The tent and everything inside it can be dismantled and packed in less than two hours.

The words underlined in the text are those Kerry chose. She then listed them on her notes page:

camel or goat hair ✓
woven ✓
sheeps ✓
Sahara ✓
rolleded up ✓
low-lying ✓
sit down ✓
two or three poles ✓

The tick after each word was added later, when, on the teacher's advice, Kerry checked that she had used all her notes in her account of the information. This account was as follows:

Bedouin tents

1 camel and goat hair is used for the tent
2 It is woven into little bit of thread
3 They sheep on rugs [Note: Kerry appeared to have written 'sleep' first, then to have changed it to 'sheep'].
4 They live in the Sahara and Travill to playse.
5 They put the rug Down
 Becauz the man and woman are separated
6 The tents are low lying
 Becauz the sand saurm migt blow Them uP
7 you can not stand uP in the tent.
 becauz it is low.
8 It has Two of Three Poles in The tent.

Kerry's teacher took a closer look at her response:

> For Kerry, the most fruitful area for exploration in connection with this task is probably Pursuit of Meaning, particularly questions concerned with using context fully, main ideas or following a (brief) line of argument. There might also be something to consider in the area of recognizing sentences, as opposed to just points of information.
>
> Kerry underlined and then listed words related to the 5 key points of information given on the first page –
>
> 1 Woven camel or goat hair.
> 2 Sheep's wool used in the Sahara.

3 Back and sides of tent can be rolled up.
4 Tents are low (so people sit).
5 Number of poles supporting tent.

In addition, in her written account of the information, Kerry referred to two further points from the second page of the text (the Bedouin travel about and the men and women are separated in the tent). She was probably helped to recall these two points by the preparatory class discussion of the text. Even so, it is clear that she has been able to recognize important vocabulary and understand several key ideas in the text. Her written account also shows some appreciation of at least one supporting point of detail – the reason for having 'low-lying' tents. (There is also some indication, though not very explicit, in 'woven into little bit of thread', that she had an idea of the long strips into which the animal hair is woven.)

Kerry's written account also raises some points which I would want to explore with her. For example, she has become confused about the role of sheep's wool in the life of the Bedouin, possibly because class discussion about how they sleep (which is not referred to in the text) has misled her; she has also misread the specific point about people normally remaining seated in the tent, possibly because the 'Although' construction which starts the sentence was unfamiliar; and, in choosing to underline and use in her account the idea of 'two or three' poles for the tent, she has missed the main point of that sentence, that the rich leader of the group would have a bigger tent. Kerry's account also raises possible points for exploration in respect of her writing, of course, if the teacher wishes to discuss them with her, or perhaps take them into account the next time they are working on 'Writing'.

A 'growth point' for Kerry is her ability to find key points as she works sequentially through the text and to recall key points from class discussion of it. Her confidence would be boosted by praise for this and she could be assured that she can become even better at noting and writing down the important information (perhaps to give to another group).

Her main need to achieve this improvement seems to be to read each information point and each sentence carefully, relating them to their immediate context. Next lesson I will take time to work with Kerry's group on this text and similar ones, helping them to look *consciously* at what comes just before and just after a point like 'In the Sahara, sheep's wool is used', to see what the *whole message* is about that point.

I might also 'box' sections of text dealing with ideas which are linked or affect one another and ask the pupils to explain the message of each 'box'. When they are used to this approach, I will invite the group to discuss and decide for themselves where the 'boxes' should be drawn; and then to decide what the 'message' of each box is.

Reflecting on the case studies

So what might we learn from the case studies? First, perhaps, that assessment in reading does not have to impose an additional burden on teachers or learners. Each case study illustrated the use of assessment evidence which came from everyday classroom activities. Second, that evidence about children's reading can come either from within the language programme or from other areas across the curriculum. The interpretation of that evidence is the key factor. Third, the case studies highlight the learner as a vital source of information without whose contribution it would be easy to misinterpret evidence and to identify inappropriate next steps in learning. In addition the evidence obtained can just as often point towards issues in teaching as to issues related to learning. Perhaps the case studies also help to demonstrate that approaches to the development of reading are the same for all learners: no matter what are the child's present abilities in reading, the process remains constant – identify what the child can do and build from there, recognizing strengths, encouraging confidence and providing practical ideas as to how progress might be made.

The case studies also portray each child's individuality and therefore the need for the teacher's professionalism, matching knowledge of each child as a person to the strategies most likely to prove successful.

At the beginning of this chapter we compared reading to the dragon in children's literature. Teachers involved in the development and implementation of the diagnostic procedures suggested that reading only remained a dragon when they were concerned about their own level of knowledge and skills. Were they supporting their pupils appropriately? Were their suggestions good suggestions? Were there other things they should have been doing? For some the package on 'Taking a Closer Look' served to reinforce existing good practice; for others it provided a framework for the analysis of evidence and acted as a source of new ideas. Different teachers used the procedures in different ways, building them into their existing practices, extending rather than radically altering their present practice. In children's literature the dragon was always overcome by someone who faced up to it and had the confidence to challenge it. It is not only children's confidence which should be our concern. Facing the reading dragon will mean boosting our own confidence as teachers. Confident teachers of reading are far more likely to encourage confident readers.

'Taking a Closer Look at Reading' is available from:

The Scottish Council for Research in Education
15 St John Street
Edinburgh
EH8 8JR

4

TEACHERS CHANGING THE SYSTEM

Alternative assessment of first graders' literacy

*Jo Worthy, James V. Hoffman, Nancy L. Roser, William
Rutherford, Sharon McKool and Susan Strecker*

The primary purpose of this chapter is to describe a grass-roots initiative in alternative assessment. A small group of first-grade teachers in Austin, Texas, approached the central administration begging for respite from the district's mandated assessment for first-graders – the *Iowa Test of Basic Skills* (ITBS). We present the story of these teachers who, with the district's blessing and with guidance from the university faculty, helped to develop and evaluate an alternative model of assessment which came to be called the Primary Assessment of Language Arts and Mathematics (PALM). Using their own words, we tell of their initial excitement and anticipation for grass-roots change, their study and research of the issues and of alternative assessment models, their implementation, piloting and evaluation of their own model, their dissemination methods and, finally, their reflections on the innovation.

Background

Because many teachers have moved away from a view of reading and writing as separate, skills-based subjects to one that encompasses the language arts as integrated and reciprocal processes, their thinking about literacy assessment has changed as well. Through such sources as in-service education, university courses, professional readings, and informal 'word-of-mouth' sharing, teachers have come to believe more strongly that they are the best judges of their children's literacy (Johnston 1987) and, further, that 'traditional assessments of literacy [most notably, standardized achievement tests] have been based on an outdated and inappropriate model of literacy' (Winograd, Paris and Bridge 1991: 108). Although many teachers recognize that traditional standardized tests tell them how well a child (or a class or school) performs in relation to a reference group, these tests provide no information about an individual's specific competencies – information that is the most useful for instruction. Further, decontextualized tests and tasks bear little or no resemblance to the authentic texts and purposeful tasks that teachers have come to rely on in their classrooms. One common corollary of system-wide assessment is that teachers feel compelled to put their regular instruction on hold while engaging their students in practice sessions that may often span several weeks.

When school systems use scores of their students on tests for teacher accountability, and when instruction doesn't match those tests, little wonder that teachers are anxious about their students' performances. This kind of assessment is seen as having high status. Increasingly, teachers themselves offer alternative proposals and arguments for assessments that reflect classroom practices as replacements for tests of isolated skills assessed in decontextualized ways. These alternatives are often given low status. This system of uneven accountability, the mixed messages about instruction and assessment, and the frustration of wasted instructional time led a group of first-grade teachers to formulate a plan of action to take some ownership of the assessment procedures in their school district.

The beginnings of change

The Austin Independent School District serves a diverse community of close to one million citizens. In the fall semester 1993, six first-grade teachers from different schools raised questions regarding the appropriateness of the ITBS as a measure of young children's literacy learning. The teachers were members of an informal network in the district who were moving toward literature-based instruction in their classrooms. After meeting repeatedly to discuss their concerns, they approached the district's central administration with a request for a waiver from standardized testing for first-graders. In petitioning for the waiver, the teachers presented arguments related to the limited utility of the ITBS both for assessing primary students' learning and for serving instructional planning. They further argued that the ITBS caused a significant disruption to their teaching schedules and produced high levels of student frustration. The Associate Superintendent expressed support for the initiative and recommended that the group prepare a plan for an alternative assessment to replace the ITBS.[1]

The teachers approached a University of Texas faculty member (one of the authors) to work beside them as they designed an alternative assessment. Members of the university faculty and district staff were already

---

1 It should be noted that the ITBS is no longer required for Austin's first-graders.

working closely together as part of a 'Language Arts Task Force' to redesign the district's language arts curriculum. From the outset, the teachers began to prepare a 'portrait' of a developing reader by searching for, adapting and blending developmental checklists from other districts, making modifications by relying on experience. Their first 'product' was a developmental profile of language, literacy and math indicators.

After a preliminary report to the school board and display of the pilot draft, the teachers received approval (in the early summer of 1994) for a one-year waiver from standardized testing in all first-grade classrooms in the district. As a condition of the waiver, however, the teachers, under the guidance of the Associate Superintendent, were charged with developing a full-scale performance-based alternative assessment model, performing a systematic evaluation of that model and proposing an implementation plan for using the model district-wide in place of the ITBS. The evaluation study was mandated for the 1994–1995 school year. Additional university-based teacher educators joined the project as collaborators.

Planning, implementing and evaluating alternative assessments

The initial planning team, consisting of the six first-grade teachers and the university-based teacher educators, began working during the summer of 1994 to formulate plans for the alternative assessment and the evaluation study. An overarching goal was to develop an assessment plan to address the needs of teachers, as well as parents, administrators, policy-makers and especially learners. One of our goals was to get rid of standardized testing. Another was to become more familiar with ways to assess. The planning team expressed their initial intentions:

- If [other] teachers ... becom[e] more aware of how to assess continually, that is probably one of the major goals. They're going to see ... what their children's needs are, where to go with them, what they can do to help them.
- One of my personal goals – if you can have personal goals for others – is to see more people become involved in assessing their children and meeting their needs.
- My expectations were to come up with something that would be an alternative assessment that would be manageable in the classroom [and] that would suit many different teaching styles.
- Our aim was to design something that was not a standardized test that would make teachers accountable and be a good assessment for the kids.
- Our job was to convince the Board that we shouldn't do what we had been doing. I got involved because the Board said we won't let you stop testing until you give us something that's better.

In late summer, a letter was sent to all the over two hundred first-grade teachers in the district explaining the goals of the PALM initiative and inviting participation in the development and piloting of an assessment model. Of the 140 teachers who expressed interest in the project by attending a preliminary meeting, a total of twenty teachers from thirteen different schools actually volunteered to participate in the planning and evaluation of an alternative assessment for the district. The twenty included four of the six teachers who had instigated the appeal for change. All twenty of these teachers administered the newly developed 'profile' to their students at the beginning of September 1994. The group then met for four day-long staff development sessions spread across the academic year to focus on further refinement of the profile, to develop a set of useful alternative assessments and to plan the evaluation study.

As developed by the collaborative team, the PALM model drew on a performance assessment perspective and emphasized the use of 'authentic' assessment strategies (Guthrie, Van Meter, Mitchell, and Reed 1994). The teachers read, conversed and debated the merits of each step in the model's development. Three types of performance assessment tasks emerged to become the framework of the PALM model:

1   Curriculum embedded assessment;
2   'Taking-a-closer-look' assessment; and
3   On-demand assessment.

Curriculum embedded assessment

Because the teacher planners insisted on finding or developing assessment tasks that mirrored instructional tasks and thus required no artificial preparation for testing, 'curriculum embedded assessments' were developed. The term simply refers to the data gathering teachers do in conjunction with their ongoing classroom instruction – thus, assessment 'embedded' in practice. As a way of monitoring students' learning and engagement with instructional tasks, the teachers proposed systematic collection and evaluation of work samples as well as observational or anecdotal notes. Responding to these data meant continuously adapting their instruction to meet student needs.

> 'It's made me a lot more organized in what I was doing and a lot more reflective. Whereas before I would take anecdotal notes or I would really be a kidwatcher, but I didn't sit back and reflect on the information that I had gathered about a particular student and didn't gain that insight.'

> 'I get notes from parents after my conferences with them saying, "I don't believe all this information you have on my child. [That

was] the most informative conference I've ever been to and I have a child in fifth grade, too." I [had] just said, "This shows what your child can do; it's not a deficit model; it's backed up by this and this and this. Now, let me show you my anecdotal records. Let me show you your child's portfolio. Let me show you the running records." I didn't have to go into the developmental profile because I said, "This is just a place for me to summarize all this other information." They just really see their kids.'

'Taking-a-closer look' assessment

The second type of performance assessment the teachers pursued for the PALM model aimed toward data that teachers typically gather as part of their in-depth study of individual learners. That is, when teachers find that they have questions about an individual student's development that cannot be adequately addressed through day-to-day instruction and assessment, a more 'close-up' inspection of the student's learning in a particular area may be necessary. Because many effective teachers already use such up-close informal assessments when they need more or different kinds of information (including informal reading inventories or running records, miscue analysis, think-alouds, and/or individual problem-solving sessions), the teachers in the study group proposed and considered several 'taking-a-closer-look' assessments.

'It just makes it so much clearer – those needs that they have and what's missing – what you didn't get when you were doing other assessments.'

'When you use the PALM, you just become more aware of every individual child and where that child is because when you're keeping your assessments up to date, you're much more aware of your kids' progress.'

On-demand assessment

The teachers also designed 'on-demand' assessments which involved data gathering within a particular time frame and under prescribed conditions, using the same tasks and materials for all participants. The 'controls' permitted monitoring the growth of individual children and made it possible to compare an individual with peers. Because demand assessments are focused on documenting and interpreting student performance on specific learning tasks, the teachers designed these tasks to reflect the kinds of learning activities that their students were already familiar with, again precluding disruption to normal learning routines. For the PALM model, the language arts demand assessments included writing in response to literature, keeping a daily journal and keeping records of information gained from nonfiction text read aloud.

'I did a little mini-workshop with kindergarten, first and second grade teachers last fall and they really liked it. They said, "Yeah! We finally got an assessment that means something, that has some credibility," and they were just excited.'

'Probably the most influential one would have been the reading response, the individual reading and having them respond to it. That was not something I had [had] them do a lot of . . . before.'

'The PALM assessments were things that I was already doing and ways that I was already assessing the children. Probably within the past five years I've gone away from the paper and pencil type of assessment.'

Teachers in the PALM group administered demand assessments to their students in the spring semester of 1994–95. The following summer, as part of the evaluation of the project, teachers and university collaborators worked together to devise scoring procedures for the reading and writing portions of the demand assessments.

The evaluation study, designed to demonstrate the effectiveness of PALM (and to show its correlation with ITBS) was completed during the summer of 1995 and was presented to the Board of Trustees the following fall. The Board approved a plan to continue the development and dissemination of PALM. Under the plan, teachers from pre-kindergarten to second grade would be invited to help in further development of the model during Year 1 (1995–96). In Year 2 (1996–97), the model would become a district mandate for all first-grade students. In Year 3 (1997–98), teachers of students from pre-kindergarten through second grade would implement the model. Meanwhile, the district would provide in-service education, workshops and teacher-to-teacher instruction of the model.

Reflections on change

As part of the evaluation study, all teachers were interviewed about their involvement in the project. One year later, the teachers were interviewed again to revisit their views about their participation in the first year and to explore their ideas about the project's second year. The following sections present the findings of those interviews.

YEAR 1: STRONG ROOTS

The end-of-year interviews in year one focused on teachers' views on standardized tests, their understanding of district and school expectations about assessment, their own views about and uses of assessments, their instructional practices, their participation in the PALM project and their views about the effectiveness of the new assessment strategies. Although most of the teachers claimed to have already used assessments similar to those in the PALM project, the majority said that the new strategies gave them a more systematic way to organize assessment and induced them to do more assessment than they had previously done.

> 'It forced me to slow down and think about my children in some detail, and to observe my children. It kinda guided my anecdotal records, particularly at the first of the year as I was getting to know my learners. I feel like I know these kids very, very well. Because we had the checklist and it was formalized as to its usage, then I absolutely *had* to do this at certain times. With anecdoctal records, so many things are important that all those important things can take over your time, and this forced me to take a real look, and then I set up a time for it in the evenings before my husband got home from work, and it was enjoyable. I'd either fix hot tea or a cup of coffee and look at my work samples and either work on the checklist or work on my anecdotals'. . . .

About half of the teachers mentioned that they had begun keeping anecdotal notes only since becoming involved in the PALM project.

While the teachers believed that principals, parents and other stakeholders continued to view standardized test scores as the major evidence of student success, they hoped the district was moving toward more authentic assessments and that the strategies used in the PALM project would be accepted as part of that change. Most teachers had used the PALM assessments in determining grades for report cards and in planning and implementing parent conferences. Those who did so reported that parents were very positive about seeing examples and evaluations of their children's work.

> 'I understand more because of PALM to some extent and because of my own reading, I understand the developmental process that the kids are tracking along so I feel like, again, I'm communicating more effectively with parents. And this year, really, I had a parent yesterday who commented, "Oh, I didn't know that's how it went." And I thought, "Yes, I'm able to inform her because of the mass of knowledge that I had." I was able to tell her how writing looks at the beginning and on and on.'

Teachers were mixed in their views about how much effect the project had on their classroom instruction. Some talked about the tremendous effect that the new strategies had in their classrooms, while others suggested that they already used familiar classroom teaching activities as 'assessment' tasks.

'When it came to portfolios and more one-on-one reading with the kids and actually annotating what they were doing, it had a great influence. When it came to, like, things I was doing in the room, like response journal and all that, it didn't at all, because I was already going to do all that. But when it came to collecting student work and making and organizing notes, it [had tremendous effect].'

'It helped with things like portfolios. I feel like I'm doing a more refined job and that helped in my planning.'

After Year 1, the teachers in the PALM evaluation study were over-whelmingly positive about their use of the PALM model and their participation in its development and evaluation. In explaining their enthu-siasm, teachers spoke about the professional 'highs' that accompany collaborating to investigate and install change:

'I've read so many books and now I've been in discussion groups and we've started one on the faculty. I probably went at it partly to help with the cause and also to learn. I was a lone person on my campus for this grade level and so I thought, "Well, it would be good to talk with other teachers".'

YEAR 2: STRUGGLES TO MAINTAIN

After the second year of the project, the teachers were interviewed again to determine how their hopes and plans for the alternative assessment had been met, their perception of the impact of the assessment model in their classrooms, the degree to which they felt the 'innovation' had been supported, and their concerns for the project if it became the mandated assessment for the district. There were both positive and negative 'themes' that emerged from inspection of the interview transcripts and notes. Each of the themes is again illustrated with the teachers' 'voices'. Major concerns during the second year interviews were:

1   The PALM model waned during the second year (due to a number of external factors). For a variety of reasons, many of the teachers felt that their second year with the alternative assessment model was less intensive than the first. They cited a variety of reasons including changes in grade assignment, demands of other innovations, reduced involvement with the network of colleagues who had installed the change, increased class size, and an uncertain audience for the results:

'Well, I have to be honest and say that I didn't feel like the PALM was going to go anywhere this year, because no one was going to look at it other than me.'

47

'I'm trying to still continue. Probably not quite as much as when I had to turn it in. I don't feel that pressure ... I guess what's missing is some of that deadline.'

2   The PALM assessment was seen as unaligned with current reporting procedures and therefore duplicated paperwork. Some teachers lamented the time demands that alternative assessments dictate, especially when unaligned with the reporting procedures already in place:

'I think a lot of teachers are just afraid that it's going to be so much work. They're wondering how much more they're going to have put on them. Will they have to do standard report cards and the PALM profile? Will it be double work?'

'The other thing is it's not in place of a report card. See, I think people are wanting something in place of the report card. And to have to do two [reporting systems] and to also have to do that numerical or letter grade report card ... I don't know. We'll see.'

[After a workshop that she presented to teachers in her school]: 'And they said, "Yeah! We finally got an assessment that means something, that has some credibility," and they were just really excited. "Now can we put away all that other stuff [report cards and other paperwork] and just do this?" And when they found out they couldn't, they got bogged down trying to do it all.'

'The administrators had me talk to [kindergarten and prekinder-garten] teachers last year about what kind of data I was getting. And they saw it as a very valuable tool. Particularly the kindergarten teachers because they felt like they didn't have anything even close to this that would help them document progress and communicate with parents. And so they were very excited. Now, we'll see as we move into it whether they'll be as excited about the record keeping part.'

'I would almost like this to be our reporting system. If we're going to be doing this and it takes a whole long time, and this is more informative than any report card we've ever used before, then this should be our reporting system. We have to tell [parents] anyway. So, if we're going to have to use this PALM with good detailed information, then this is what we should be telling them. This would encourage me to want to do it, because then I would see it going somewhere.'

3   The further teachers were from the development of this innovation, the less understanding and commitment they felt. Although teachers were the primary wielders of change in this model for alternative assessment,

they discovered that some of their colleagues were as hesitant to become involved as if the change had been mandated externally (Erickson 1995):

'Somehow these other teachers have to feel some ownership, too. And I'm not sure how.'

'There are going to be some really gung ho, there are going to be some who will participate because they're supposed to, there are going to be some who gripe all the way. No different from anything else. There are a lot of people who see the positives who just don't want to fool with it because they don't want to take the time.'

'I think there're going to be problems. I think people won't be ready for it emotionally or philosophically. . . . Those who have changed their philosophy, have changed the way they operate in the classroom, will have a little better understanding of what they're doing. Others, I think, will just fill it out. If they *have* to.'

'There are people who see this as the pet project of those few who started it. They don't agree with the philosophy and they don't like it.'

'It gets at the notion of time and engagement and what is yours.'

4   Teachers felt that changes that are mandated are replete with the same problems as the ITBS. Although the teachers varied somewhat in the degree to which they thought a huge school district *must* 'mandate' alternative assessments for all primary students, they agreed strongly that mandates will not work to effect real change:

'I'm watching our teachers. We're having to go through curriculum alignment. See how I use the phrase, "having to", which I'm sure people will use in this context. I don't always have time to think about [innovations] in that kind of depth. Our principal has so little time, too, and he says, "Oh, please, why doesn't the district just give us something? It would be so much faster." And I thought about all the shelves of things that I have that the district has given me.'

'I just think it's a shame that it can't also be the progress report to parents. Because when it comes down to it, I think teachers are going to be real bitter about having to do that and report to the parents. It's a double duty.'

'I just don't know if the district will follow through. It just seems like our district has a reputation for starting things and then if somebody else waves something in the air, they go with that.'

'I feel worried about the mandate. Other teachers ask me, "What's going to happen? What does it mean?" They fear it's another thing they're going to be required to do.'

'I don't think it should be mandated at all. I think that you're gonna get a lot of resistance and then once again, it's gonna destroy the model, which is a very positive, wonderful model. It will be misunderstood and people [will] feel resentful – another thing to *have* to do. And if things go the way they're going, I just have this terrible feeling that in about two years, we'll be back to the ITBS. I really do. Because the teachers are gonna say, "Oh, my god, ITBS is three days. It's so easy; it tells me what to say. I know my kids. I don't need to do all this." I can see a meeting with teachers petitioning to go back to ITBS.'

Positive indicators of teachers' working collaboratively toward more defensible assessments of children's literacy also emerged from the second-year interviews:

1 Teachers became more systematic and reflective in their assessment procedures and record-keeping. Even teachers who viewed themselves as effective in their record-keeping and reporting indicated that the 'system' they imposed upon themelves through the alternative assessment in the PALM model affected their practice:

'I was already doing the record keeping. It probably helped me keep on track more.'

'I was more systematic in what I was doing.'

'I use it more as a tool (as it was meant to be), as an evaluation and assessment tool. Last year, I was using it as part of my ongoing learning about my own practice. This year, I came in and I was already organized. The striking thing is that it's helped me a whole lot with my kindergarten kids. Watching their growth and being able to document their growth and so on. And I felt like, again, I have accurate things to say.'

'It also helped with things like portfolios. I feel I'm doing a more refined job and that helped me in planning for this year.'

'The way it influenced me is that it made me a lot more organized in what I was doing and a lot more reflective. Whereas before I would take the anecdotal notes or I would really be a kidwatcher, but I didn't sit back and reflect on the information that I had gathered about a particular student and didn't gain that insight. That's where the PALM has really focused me. There's that reflective component that I ha[d] been missing out on. And it also helped me to manage what I was doing more clearly and not so haphazardly.'

Although only a few teachers were using all components of the PALM, all said they had benefited from their involvement. Most were using instructional and assessment approaches they had learned from PALM and some spoke of having more awareness of how to assess students in general.

2   Teachers learned a lot in the process of instituting change.
Perhaps an important part of any change is the process of change itself; in the case of PALM, the meetings, reading and collegiality became benefits to the participants:

> 'What comes to me is the reflective practice that we went through where we listened to you and others talk about practices and then y'all promoted the discussions among us.'

> 'I felt much more solid and it really did help me to have the co-workers to bounce ideas off of and to say, okay, this is what's going on in other schools. And then I realized, yes, I am on track on some things or I'm comfortable with what I'm doing. It gave me some support.'

> '[I miss the support in the second year], the support from the University and from the district. It was more than just giving us the instrument and saying, "Go for it; see what you can get out of it." The networking was more an informal system. You had to contact who you wanted to talk to.'

3   There was some positive feeling about the innovation being mandated.
Critically important precepts and understandings become a 'have to do'. People become involved in spite of themselves. Most typically, reformers involved with grass-roots change resist the imposition of mandate, even if what is 'mandated' is the reform they instituted. Nevertheless, many of these teachers thought they saw the necessity for systematizing the gathering of information from young readers – and viewed the district's mandate for the PALM as one reasonable way to ensure those systematic data:

> 'I really do think from time to time that if the district says, "You will," it helps. Because I think that when people look at it, I really do think people will see the quality there. Maybe I'm naive; I hope not. I really hope people will say, "Oh, this speaks to what I see about children, and this meshes with our program goals."'

> 'If it is implemented and supported, then it will be great. It has great potential especially to strengthen the ties between grade levels because it makes the transition easier for students and teachers if [first grade teachers] know that this child can do these things already or could at the end of kindergarten.'

'On the mandate, I think it's necessary. I think there needs to be some type of standardization. There's a lot of work on the curriculum alignment, but I think there needs to be something that can go with the child from school to school with all the moves.'

'I think it's way past time there was a mandate because isolated teachers in isolated classrooms – the PALM really benefits that particular class. But until everybody's using it, it can't really do a lot.'

4   Teachers recognized many strategies. Repeatedly, the teachers informed us that the assessments in the PALM model were not new to them; they had, in fact, always included this array of assessment in their own classroom planning and assessment. Even so, they typically mentioned one or two practices that stretched them:

'I already did all this except for the literature response journals. We hadn't written about our reading in quite that way.'

'I already did all these things in my classrooms, except perhaps for the running records. I found those interesting and informative.'

'All of this stuff was comfortable for me. It didn't change a lot of what I was doing except maybe literature response.'

We viewed the 'we already did all this' as perhaps the most positive indicator that grass-roots changes reflected the roots of teacher practice. How extraordinary it would be to find that teachers who designed reform felt it necessary to be schooled in their own reform. Within the literature on teacher 'change', the notion that 'we already did this' is often construed as resistance or lack of understanding. Within the struggles for grass-roots change, 'we already did this' means comfort, buy-in, familiarity and allegiance. Importantly, the word 'except' signals openness to 'doing it' better, more carefully, more knowingly, more collaboratively, and more reflectively.

In professional journals, teachers are told that effective assessment is *a*) continuous and inseparable from instruction, *b*) multi-dimensional and *c*) authentic, and that it should occur in a variety of formats and contexts (see review in Tompkins and McGee, 1993). Surely, this grass-roots effort for early assessment reform met these criteria. Further, because 'change' came from the teachers themselves, they were both strengthened by the process and aligned with its result. Nevertheless, when 'roots' spread, there is no guarantee that they will be as deep or as strong as their 'parent'. These teachers, then, having created an alternative that was to become the 'mandated assessment,' met all the resistance of any 'top down' decree. They were embroiled in the reality of change and struggling to maintain the (grass) roots.

Changing practice

Lessons can be learned from this project about changing practice in literacy assessment:

- when teachers feel that the assessment systems they are required to use do not properly demonstrate their children's developing abilities, then change can occur at a system-wide level if teachers have a commitment to changing that system.
- collegiality – meetings, discussion of strategies and protocols, trial and error practice, and acceptance that revision will always be necessary – is a key to teacher empowerment in this area.
- the closer teachers are to the change process and to the initiation of that process the greater the commitment to change will be.
- involvement in changing practice in literacy assessment can lead to teachers becoming more reflective of their practice generally.
- there are very obvious benefits for the professional self-esteem of teachers, as well as for parents and students, in a system of literacy assessment that encourages teachers to articulate the progress of individual children.

References

Argyris, C. (1985) *Strategy, Change and Defensive Routines,* London: Pitman Publishers Inc.

Erickson, L.G. (1995) *Supervision of Literacy Program: Teachers as Grass-roots Change Agents,* Boston: Allyn-Bacon.

Farr, R. (1992) 'Putting it all together: Solving the reading assessment puzzle', *The Reading Teacher* 46: 26–37.

Fullan, M. (with Stiegelbauer, S.) (1991) *The New Meaning of Educational Change,* New York: Teachers College Press.

Guthrie, J., Van Meter, P., Mitchell, A. and Reed, C. (1994) 'Performance assessments in reading and language arts', *The Reading Teacher* 48: 266–71.

Johnston, P. (1987) 'Teachers as evaluation experts', *The Reading Teacher* 40: 744–8.

Kirkpatrick, D.L. (1985) *How to Manage Change Effectively,* San Francisco: Jossey-Bass Inc.

Tompkins, G.E. and McGee, L.M. (1993) *Teaching Reading with Literature: Case Studies to Action Plans,* New York: Macmillan.

Winograd, P., Paris, S. and Bridge, C. (1993). 'Improving the assessment of literacy', *The Reading Teacher* 45: 108–16.

5

LITERACY ASSESSMENT AS PART OF NEW STANDARDS

P. David Pearson, Elizabeth Spalding
and Miles Myers

This chapter is a description of the work of the Literacy Unit of the New Standards Project, a US-based voluntary association of states and school districts committed to the reform of America's schools through the development of high standards for all students in science, mathematics and the English language arts and rigorous assessment systems that will allow all stakeholders in the enterprise to monitor progress toward achieving those standards. Make no mistake about it: New Standards is in the business of building high stakes assessments. Once a rigorous programme of research and development, a programme involving all the partners and appropriate content area experts, has produced these standards and assessments, New Standards intends to use them to drive school reform and restructuring efforts among its member schools. The basic idea is to hold every student, every teacher and every school – not just the privileged ones – to high and rigorous standards. In return for holding themselves to account, so the logic goes, schools will receive the curricular, material and professional development resources needed to support all students and teachers in meeting those standards.

Getting started: some background about New Standards

The New Standards Project, or as it has recently been dubbed, New Standards, is the brain child of Lauren Resnick of the Learning, Research and Development Center at the University of Pittsburgh, and Mark Tucker of the Center for Education and the Economy, Washington, DC. As of press time for this book, New Standards was comprised of twenty-four partners, including seventeen states and seven large school districts. It derives its funding from several sources: foundation grants, in-kind contributions from various units and dues from its member partners. For a period of five years (1991–1996), New Standards contracted with the National Council of Teachers of English (NCTE) to carry out the work of the New Standards Literacy Unit. Prior to NCTE's entry into the project, the work of the Literacy Unit was directed by Barbara Kapinus, who is currently with the Council of Chief State School Officers in Washington, DC, and Daniel Resnick of Carnegie Mellon University.

Curricular integration as a goal for language arts. Kapinus and Resnick, bolstered by the advice, support and good work of several literacy educators, were responsible for the conception that schools needed to examine reading and writing as complementary elements under the general rubric of literacy. While this conceptualization remains a long-term goal, we must confess that we have not yet fully achieved it in the work of the Literacy Unit; we, along with the teachers with whom we work, seem to be more comfortable with separate indices of reading and writing competence.

Assessment as a reform tool. New Standards has been quite open about its intent to use assessment as the engine of reform in our schools. Not everyone agrees, of course, that assessment should be used to force school reform. Nevertheless, most educators acknowledge the fact that K–12 curricula have been designed to cater to the dominant form of assessment in our schools, which for the last fifty years has been the multiple choice test. Both assessment and instruction, then, have been organized around decomposition of tasks into small bits and literal meaning:

> Therefore, drill on materials that closely resemble tests is accepted as a legitimate and effective means to improve achievement ... psychometricians have been center stage in the development process, defining the rules of test making and compiling the final instrument. ... If subject-matter experts had always had equal say, how can we imagine that teachers of English would have given up essay tests in deference to rater-judge reliability coefficients? (Shepard 1993:11–12)

Lauren and Daniel Resnick (1992), in building the conceptual framework for New Standards, concluded that the problem is not that teachers teach to the test but that teachers need tests worth teaching too. Noting that narrowly conceived tests have helped create a curriculum crisis in the schools, many researchers have called for broader, more challenging assessments to encourage restructuring of our schools and to shift the curriculum goals of schools to a different form of literacy (Wiggins 1993). To meet this challenge, New Standards has undertaken the task of developing, through tasks and portfolios, new assessments of performance in reading, speaking, writing, science and mathematics. These assessments are to be based on the curriculum content standards emerging from the various professional efforts. For the Literacy Unit, this has involved studying the draft versions of the content standards jointly developed by the National Council of Teachers of English/International Reading Association and translating them into performance standards for reading, writing, speaking and listening.

New Standards has been guided in its work by a compact signed by the original partners in New Standards. This contract has allowed research and development to be protected from the immediate demands for reporting scores for individual students. The compact commits all New Standards personnel to the principle that no individual scores will be reported by New Standards until all users of New Standards materials have provided full and complete support, which translates into resources and appropriate curriculum, for individual students attempting to attain a passing score. In addition, New Standards has insisted that assessments used for individual high stakes reporting must be a) based upon portfolio evidence b) meet acceptable psychometric requirements and c) emanate from accepted subject-matter standards. Therefore, the entire focus of New Standards over its first four or five years has been research and development. During that time, no state or district has used New Standards assessments to produce individual scores. But New Standards is entering a period in which it will become dependent on the production and marketing of its materials to sustain its operations. It remains to be seen whether future clients and purchasers of assessment materials will abide by the compact as a condition of using New Standards assessment materials. The danger, of course, is that high and rigorous standards accompanied by challenging assessments but unaccompanied by equally challenging curriculum and rich resources could become a cruel hoax for students and parents, especially those who regard schools as the one institution in our society which provides hope for improving their lot in life.

A short history of the research and development programme of New Standards

New Standards has journeyed through several phases of research and development in its relatively short history. Throughout its history, involvement of classroom teachers has always been one of New Standards' guiding principles, and we believe that New Standards has been highly successful in implementing this principle. By involving thousands of teachers in assessment development, New Standards has made a major contribution in improving the teaching profession's knowledge of assessment issues. About 6,000 K–12 teachers across the country have been involved in New Standards at one time or another, attending national, regional or partner meetings or experimenting with materials and processes in the classroom as New Standards has moved through several stages of development.

Stage 1:
Easing into performance tasks

In the first stage of New Standards Literacy Unit, teachers from New Standards partners were brought together to develop on-demand tasks requiring a writing sample and open-ended responses to a reading task; these on-demand tasks are very similar to those developed under state sponsorship in California and later in Maryland and Wisconsin. Responses to these tasks from hundreds of schools were scored in 1992 by 120 teachers from across the country. This initial work introduced the idea of performance assessment, along with its traditions and constructs (rubrics, scoring guides, anchor papers, commentaries and the like) to thousands of teachers, thereby establishing the New Standards goal and message as a serious endeavour; additionally, this work carried with it the implication that New Standards was a teacher-based movement.

Stage 2:
Taking task development seriously

In the second stage of New Standards, starting in the fall of 1992, thousands of teachers were brought together from across the country to expand and refine the on-demand performance tasks and to experiment with various ways of scoring tasks and reporting results. In this stage, the goal was to create tasks that engaged students in challenging, integrated language arts curriculum events. Task development required that teachers

1 find reading selections which would elicit engagement from fourth-, eighth- and tenth-graders;
2 develop and pilot prompts challenging the reader to think about the reading selection(s) at several levels;
3 develop writing prompts with a variety of modes and rhetorical settings;
4 develop rubrics and scoring procedures for piloted tasks, including experiments with both holistic and analytic scoring procedures;
5 locate and validate student papers that vividly illustrated each level of performance defined by the rubric, and
6 prepare interpretative commentaries for these anchor papers as a way of building a communal discourse about what counts as accomplishment within this framework.

During this stage there were experiments with various types of scoring and processes for certifying judges.

The overall goal of on-demand task development in New Standards was (and still is) to develop a large task-pool sampling the domain of English and English language arts. The completed tasks include several important features:

- texts that provide rich and appropriate challenges to students' thinking;
- prompts to elicit rich reading and writing performances;
- rubrics describing, in a general way, the elements of performance that characterize different levels of accomplishment;
- anchor papers illustrating the levels;
- scoring commentaries drawing relationships between rubrics and anchor papers.

The tasks were designed to give teachers a set of widely discussed and elaborated performance indicators which they could use both to assess their own standards (by comparing these indicators with their own assessment tasks and practices), to compare their students to a nationally benchmarked set of standards (by comparing local papers with national benchmark, or anchor, papers) and to critique national standards themselves. The benchmark papers allow students to rate their own performance and to critique national scoring procedures. Viewed from another perspective, the task development was also an effort to render open and transparent for public scrutiny the practices of ranking, scoring and evaluating which occur every day in our classrooms, via classroom assignments, norm-referenced standardized tests, and criterion-referenced tests. An analysis of a sample multiple day performance task is presented in a later section entitled, 'Anatomy of a multiple-day performance task'.

During the 1993–94 academic year, New Standards conducted a major field trial of these on-demand tasks. During the summer of 1994, hundreds of teachers from around the country met to benchmark and later score these tasks as part of the process of training them to return to their states and districts and train thousands of peers, at local sites, in the same processes.

Stage 3:
Portfolio development

The third stage of New Standards, the work to develop portfolios (or as Lauren Resnick initially labelled them, records of cumulative accomplishment), began in the Literacy Unit with a 1993 Minneapolis Conference that brought together the expertise of educators in at least a dozen sites which had been implementing portfolio assessment for several years. Based on the recommendations of these experts, we selected twenty-one sites (some were long-standing New Standards schools and some were schools that had no history whatsoever with New Standards) across the country to act as consultants and experimental sites for developing foundation materials for starting a nationwide portfolio system.

Working with these teachers during the 1993–94 school year, we met three times for periods of 3–5 days. In these meetings, broken into elementary, middle, and high school groups, we began by sharing experiences and perspectives on portfolio work. Then we negotiated a plan for collaboration. In October, we agreed on a menu of artefacts that we would all use to organize student portfolios between October and February. In February, we met again to examine one another's partial portfolios in order to determine whether we were speaking a common language as we tried to find artefacts that fit our menu categories. Then we bootstrapped the initial draft of a portfolio scoring rubric, a tool for evaluating the material that we would bring back to the table in May at our third meeting. The process of developing a rubric was informative because while it failed as a rubric, it did help us clarify what ought to be in the menu; that is, we were able to answer the question, 'What should we bring to the table in May if we are really serious about using this rubric to evaluate student growth and accomplishment?'

Our task in May was threefold. First, in the interim between February and May, we had come to realize that our rubrics were not ready to use for scoring anything; several of us worked on revising our rubrics. Second, since this core of sixty-three teachers, in July 1994, were going to train 400 more teachers to participate in our 1994–95 Portfolio Assessment Field Trial, we worked on materials to aid us in the training. Third, we came to the realization that if we were ever really going to build a publicly workable and defensible portfolio system, we had to be able to communicate our intentions beyond the professional community, to parents, policy-makers, administrators, and most importantly, the real clients in all of this, the students in our schools. Thus a group of us worked on the development of student handbooks, one each for the grade four, grade eight and grade ten field trials. We settled on the student handbook as a centrepiece of our training materials because we were betting that if we could figure out a way to make the system transparent to our 'clients', to the students who would have to put it together, then communicating with parents, policy-makers, and the public would be a breeze.

We developed our rubric and used it to score a sizeable sample of portfolios, and on that sample, employing well-trained teachers who had helped to develop the rubric, we achieved about 85 per cent interjudge reliability on direct matches on a 1–4 scale. We prepared materials for our July training session; more important, the teachers who came to that meeting went back to their partner sites and trained another 2,500 teachers, all of whom later participated in our 1994–95 field trial. And we were nearing closure on drafts of three student handbooks for preparing a New Standards portfolio.

Coming out of our summer 1994 conference, we were pretty well set on two of three elements that we knew we would need, with a third still under development. The first component was a set of standards which described desirable student performance for reading, writing and oral language. Descriptions were similar, but not identical, across grade levels (elementary, middle and high school). The second was a menu outlining required and optional entries in the portfolio. For example, all students were required to include a log of books read throughout the year as well as an essay in which they had responded to a piece of literature. Additionally, students were required to include an entry demonstrating their growth as writers throughout the year; but they and their teachers could exercise substantial prerogative in determining exactly what to include in this growth entry. The third component, the student handbook, was still in draft form in July.

The 1994–95 school year proved to be a period of trial and error (and tribulation) in negotiating this approach to portfolio assessment. The standards were revised at least three different times, as was the menu of entries to guide portfolio construction. The student handbook proved an illusive goal. A final version was not available until October and, ironically, it proved more problematic than it was worth. Also during 1994–95, a decision was made to add one on-demand task to the portfolios of all students in the national sample. It would serve as an audit mechanism, a way of calibrating consistency in the application of standards across sites.

In spite of the frenetic pace of refinement and revision, which was prompted almost entirely by the desire of New Standards leadership to work out enough bugs so that the 1995–96 system would be closer to a 'real' accountability assessment, the teachers and students managed to carry out a remarkably successful portfolio assessment trial during the 1994–95 school year. Toward the end of the school year, the teachers met in partner level groups to evaluate portfolios and to select ten candidate benchmark portfolios to forward to a national benchmarking conference in July 1995. At the July conference, several important goals were accomplished. First, the teachers selected sets of portfolios which they felt adequately illustrated the type of work that would have to be submitted in order to demonstrate that a student had 'met the standard', which turned out to be a score of 4 on a 1 to 4 point scale. Second, they selected other portfolios that they felt illustrated other levels within the system. Third, they outlined the sorts of changes that would have to be made in the training materials in order to make the system more usable for teachers and students than the 1994–95 system proved to be. Some of the revised materials are shared in a later section entitled 'The current portfolio system'.

Stage 4:
Multiple assessment strategies

Responding to a variety of constituents' concerns (e.g. the time-intrusive character of performance tasks [lots of time for very little information], the difficulty and expense of scoring performance tasks and portfolios, the lack of domain coverage permitted by either performance tasks or port-folios, and the lacklustre record of both portfolios and performance tasks when subjected to conventional measurement indices), New Standard leaders decided in the fall of 1994 to add a reference examination com-ponent to the 'portfolio' of examination materials available for use by its partners.

Currently there are three components of the reference examination – a multiple-choice component and a 'short' (one-day, one-hour) performance task. The multiple-choice component looks remarkably similar to the short-passage-followed-by-several(8–10)-multiple-choice-items format so familiar in the United States in commercially-available standardized tests and often used in statewide assessments. Most of the forms of the multiple-choice reading assessment are accompanied by some of the traditional, and roundly criticized, multiple-choice editing questions (what word is inappropriate in line 17?). The short tasks appear in three distinct forms:

1   one-hour direct writing assessment prompts of the type that have become a staple in statewide assessments and college placement exam-inations (to determine English placement);
2   one-hour reading assessments in which students read a 'classic' short story or a substantial piece of expository text and respond to open-ended questions of the same variety as appear in most multiple-day reading assessments;
3   a combined reading and writing assessment in which the available hour is split between reading and answering open-ended questions and responding to a text-related writing prompt.

While some of us in the project viewed this development as a retreat from the original purpose and zeal of New Standards, there is no question about the importance of these new components in meeting two very serious criticisms of the earlier materials – poor domain coverage (are you sure you are getting at all of the important components of the language arts curriculum?) and lacklustre psychometric characteristics (do you even have enough 'scores' or 'items' to produce a stable index of language arts perfor-mance?). More later on the costs and benefits of this development. Now to an examination of the materials themselves.

New Standards assessment materials

We discuss here the three major approaches to assessment currently in the New Standards 'assessment bank' as of the time that this paper was written: performance tasks, portfolios and reference examinations.

New Standards did not begin with a template for creating a good performance task; rather the characteristics emerged over time as tasks were piloted, reviewed, revised, or discarded. Some of the principles which have emerged as guideposts for task development and revision include:

- literacy is presented in many varieties and contexts, including literary, informational, practical and persuasive modes;
- literacy includes reading, writing, listening, speaking and sometimes viewing;
- students respond both as individuals and in groups;
- assessments extend over more than one class period, to provide an opportunity for more complex and integrated responses;
- assessments over several class periods show coherence in theme and activity;
- responses are open-ended; students construct their own responses, with explicit guidelines;
- texts and situations are as authentic as possible;
- texts and examination questions are not only as free of cultural bias as possible, but promote respect for different cultures;
- students are offered some choice in what they will write;
- assessments place demands on creative thinking; and
- assessments encourage good instructional practice and rich curricula.

(New Standards, Task Development Packet 1994)

The task analysed below, Mummies and Pyramids, was designed according to these principles. It was first piloted in fall 1992 as a fourth-grade task. Over the next two years, the task went through several cycles of revisions and re-piloting, eventually becoming an eighth-grade task. The version described in this paper is the version that was administered in fall 1994 to all eighth graders (approximately 15,000) participating in the first-year field trial of the New Standards English Language Arts Portfolio. After undergoing professional and community reviews, Mummies and Pyramids was selected from a pool of tasks for use in the field trial. Fourth- and tenth-graders participating in the 1994 field trial completed similar performance tasks.

In the context of the portfolio field trial, Mummies and Pyramids was intended to 'anchor' the portfolio. That is, it served as a common task in all middle school portfolios. In addition, it was intended to be a tool for monitoring the system for equity and for certifying the authenticity of the work in a portfolio. In other words, a portfolio with a high overall score and a low score on this task might be flagged for reconsideration.

The task had several components:

- a Teacher Guide, which contained guidelines for administration, information on how the task would be scored and suggested schedules for each day including time allotments for various activities;
- a Student Response Booklet, which contained a preview of the task, general criteria by which reading and writing responses would be scored, pages for note-taking, open-ended questions on the readings and space to answer them, the writing prompt with space for a first and a revised draft, and an evaluation of the task to be completed by each student at the end of administration;
- a Reader, which consisted of excerpts from books on ancient Egypt, together with illustrations and photographs;
- a magazine, *Kids Discover Pyramids*, for each student to use as a resource in completing the task;
- a video, *Mummies Made in Egypt*, to be viewed by the class.

In addition, each classroom set of the task contained bookmarks for each student on which were printed the general criteria by which reading and writing would be scored, Peer Review Sheets which teachers could distribute to help students critique one another's drafts, and an evaluation of the task to be completed by the teacher.

The content of the task was designed to be administered over five class periods. A day-by-day description follows:

Day One: Students received an overview of the whole task, including an introduction to the writing prompt, and expectations regarding their performance. The whole class discussed what they already knew about mummies and pyramids and students completed a T-chart in their student response booklets. Throughout the task, students were encouraged to add to the T-chart as their knowledge increased. The whole class watched the video *Mummies Made in Egypt* and students took notes in their booklets.

Day Two: Each student received a *Kids Discover Pyramids* magazine. Students were given about thirty minutes to browse the magazine and take notes. Students then answered four open-ended questions about their reading.

Day Three: Students were instructed to choose one of two writing prompts:

A. Dr Mary Carter is an archaeologist who is studying how the ancient pyramids of Egypt were built. She is considering hiring a few young people to travel with her team and help with the work. Write her a persuasive letter which will convince her that your knowledge about pyramids makes you a person she should hire. Give details and be specific.

B. Dr Mary Carter is thinking of writing a book for young people about mummies. She is trying to decide what to include in her book. Write a letter telling her what information you think she should use. Make sure you include facts and information which you found the most interesting and explain why this information would be fascinating to young people.

Students then selected articles in the Reader which would help them respond to the writing prompt and took notes on their reading.

Day Four: Students finished reading and taking notes and wrote the first draft of the letter to Dr Mary Carter.

Day Five: Students shared first drafts with classmates and wrote revised drafts.

Tasks were mailed to schools in mid-October 1994. Teachers were asked to return to the Literacy Unit a selected number of copies of completed student response booklets by early January. All students were asked to place their completed booklets inside their portfolios to be scored in partner meetings at a later date. The booklets sent to the Literacy Unit were used to compile scoring training materials, which were mailed to partners in the spring of 1995. The illustrative student responses in the sections which follow were selected from these scoring training materials.

Scoring reading and writing

New Standards' task scoring system evolved as the tasks evolved. At various national meetings, several scoring systems were tried: analytic, holistic and a combination of the two dubbed 'anaholistic'. By the first large-scale task scoring, which took place in July 1993, New Standards had reached consensus that each task should receive one reading score and one writing score. Scoring of reading and writing was holistic and a six-point scale was used to describe the work: 5 – exceeds the standard; 4 – meets the standard; 3 – needs revision; 2 – additional instruction is needed; 1 – a significant amount of instruction is needed; 0 – no evidence of attempt to respond.

The holistic reading rubric used to score was developed, applied and revised over the course of several cycles of task piloting, benchmarking, and trial scoring. This reading rubric was used to score reading at each of the targeted New Standards grade levels: 4, 8 and 10. In addition, the same rubric was used to score all reading tasks, whether the texts were informational, literary, or procedural.

The rubric is based on three key, interrelated features of responses: Response Completeness, Complexity and Risk Taking (New Standards 1993). These features are implicit in the more detailed descriptors used to characterize the various levels of responses. A description of score level 4 (meets the standard) is given in Figure 5.1.

Figure 5.1 New Standards grade level 4: reading descriptors

Level 4 responses meet the standard.

The student's responses accomplish the task and the quality of performance is good. Responses are complex and demonstrate a thorough understanding and interpretation of the text. There is considerable evidence of extension of the text, such as connections to other texts, experiences, or concepts. They may even connect to their larger cultural community.

Readers at this level begin to take risks as readers.

There may be evidence of "reading like a writer" – attending to, evaluating, or appreciating the author's perspective and craft in creating the text. They pose questions, take exception, agree, disagree, and speculate. They may challenge the validity of the author's perspective by taking into account the author's authority and 'license' to address these issues or the credibility of sources used. There may also be evidence of exploring multiple meanings and evaluating alternative interpretations of events or motivations. They may develop new insights as their reading and reflection progresses.

Key descriptors: Interpretation
Personal connections
Extensions
Taking risks*
Challenging the author*
Insightful

(New Standards, 1993)

When scoring reading, scorers were instructed to read the entire performance before assigning a reading score. The 'entire performance' in the task included students' responses to the writing prompt, since the prompts were designed to elicit information about the reading students had done. Scorers were instructed to look for evidence of reading wherever they might find it, including notes, marginalia and graphics. Finally, scorers were told to think of the rubric as a menu, not a checklist – not every feature listed above need be present in every response.

An exemplary student response which represents a level 4 performance in reading appears in Appendix A. The commentary which accompanies the response links it to the rubric and elaborates on specific features of the performance.

Like the New Standards reading rubric, the writing rubrics evolved over time. Unlike the reading rubric, writing rubrics were designed to be task-specific. That is, each rubric was slightly different depending on the nature of the writing prompt. For example, specific to the task, it was noted that

Figure 5.2 New Standards grade level 4: writing descriptors

The student's responses meet the standard. The writing:

Focus/coherence
- Focuses on main points or central ideas that are often identified in the introduction, even if the writer does not divide the paper into paragraphs;
- Maintains unity and coherence with smooth transitions from one idea to the next;
- Usually engages the reader at both the beginning and end, and acknowledges the writer's purpose.

Exploration of ideas
- Supports the main points with numerous relevant and specific details;
- Supports ideas effectively by explaining their significance, making inferences, and/or drawing conclusions;
- Provides information that is generally correct with few, if any, inaccuracies.

Voice
- Shows that the writer's persona emerges through use of personal observations, responses and/or reactions;
- Often includes intensifiers and/or words with emotional connotations, and rich, fluent language.

Control of conventions
- Demonstrates clear control of writing conventions;
- Is not necessarily mechanically perfect, but errors are few, relative to length and complexity;
- Has correct, appropriate, and varied sentence structure.

Key descriptors: Focused
Coherent
Specific
Fluent
Sophisticated

---

score point 2 papers shared the characteristic of being 'information dumps'. Therefore this characteristic was incorporated into the writing scoring rubric. The major dimensions (Focus/Coherence, Exploration of Ideas, Voice, Control of Conventions) remained constant across all writing rubrics. The specific descriptors beneath each heading were customized to each task. A description of a level 4 performance is given in Figure 5.2.

An exemplary student response which represents a level 4 performance in writing appears in Appendix B. The commentary which accompanies the writing links it to the rubric and elaborates on specific features of the piece.

All teachers who administered the task were asked to return to the Literacy Unit four to six student booklets which represented a range of student performance in the classroom. Teachers were supplied with draft scoring rubrics to help them make their selections. From the booklets sent to the Literacy Unit, scoring training materials were compiled and sent to partner states and districts so that they could score the tasks when convenient.

As the first year of the portfolio field trial drew to a close, most partners found they had little time to devote to scoring tasks. Scoring and selecting portfolios for the national benchmarking turned out to be a monumental task. Partners were asked to submit a sample of scored portfolios containing scored tasks to the Literacy Unit in preparation for the national portfolio benchmarking meeting scheduled for July 1995. Most of the partners managed to score the tasks that accompanied the benchmark portfolios.

Unfortunately, a number of factors converged to obscure any clear conclusions about the value of the tasks as portfolio 'anchors'. Among them were:

- Because of time constraints, many partners did not 'blind' score the tasks. They scored them after the portfolios had already been scored and a subset of those portfolios had been selected as benchmark, or exemplary, portfolios.
- At the national portfolio benchmarking meeting, attendees (about ten participants per grade level) spent all their time benchmarking the portfolios and had no time left for systematic examination of the anchor tasks.
- Many teachers who administered the tasks were critical of the length of time required to complete the task and the overall logistics of administering a complex task.
- The cost to New Standards of preparing, printing and mailing the anchor tasks was high, as was the preparation, printing and mailing of anchor task scoring training materials. New Standards decided to reduce costs by dropping the anchor tasks from the portfolio system, at least for the time being.

The Literacy Unit did discover some unexpected uses for the anchor tasks. First, although they were not instructed to do so, many middle school students selected all or part of the task as one of their portfolio entries. They identified the entries in a variety of ways: some students used the task as evidence of reading; some used it as evidence of persuasive writing or report writing. This suggests that the anchor task did perform a valuable function for some students by helping them fill gaps in their portfolios. Second, the task yielded unexpected evidence of opportunity-to-learn. That is, we reviewed a number of portfolios which contained mostly highly structured, teacher-generated assignments (for example, Write a paragraph using at least eight proper nouns). In these portfolios, much of the writing was formulaic, constrained and not engaging. Often, the anchor task provided the best source of evidence that the student could meet the standards in reading and writing, given the opportunity. Finally, we received many positive evaluations of the task from both students and teachers. Many students told us how much they enjoyed both the topic and the activities of the task. Many teachers stated that the task had provided them with a positive model for curriculum and instruction, that it had allowed them the opportunity to act as observers in their own classrooms, and to discover students' previously unseen strengths and weaknesses (Spalding 1995a).

At the time of going to press, the future of multiple-day performance tasks in New Standards is unclear. Since their capacity to serve as an auditing device for the validity of portfolio scores has never been examined, it is unlikely that they will survive on those grounds. And now that the reference exam is in place, it may, because of its more protracted scope, serve that same function at a much lower cost, in terms of administration and scoring time.

The current portfolio system

Although performance tasks were the focus of New Standards' initial research and development work, New Standards has maintained its vision of creating a portfolio-based assessment system. The New Standards portfolio pilot year (1993–1994) and the first year field trial (1994–1995) are described in detail elsewhere (Spalding 1995b). The section which follows describes the portfolio system as it evolved in 1995–1996, the second and final year of field trial.

Figure 5.3 English language assessment

Middle grades table of contents

Reading exhibit
Evidence of quantity, range, and depth.
　Your teacher's certification of what you've read, with evidence (e.g. reading logs) attached.
Evidence of reading accomplishment.
　Literature;
　and two entries selected from: informational texts, public documents, and functional documents.

Writing exhibit
Writing accomplishment (4 entries total).
At least one entry from Category A:
A response to literature
A demonstration of proficiency in a literary genre

continued . . .

A narrative report
At least one entry from Category B:
A report
A narrative procedure
A persuasive essay
A free pick (could be from Categories A or B, but doesn't have to be).
Evidence of control of writing conventions.
 One entry slip that refers the reader to two pieces of writing in your writing exhibit.
Evidence of the use of processes and strategies for writing.
 One entry slip that refers the reader to a piece of writing in your writing exhibit, with drafts and revisions attached.

Speaking, listening and viewing exhibit
Informal speaking and listening.
 Teacher certification.
Speaking accomplishment.
 Gathering and reporting information.
 Influencing the opinions of others.
Viewing (optional).

Reflective essay
For this exhibit, prepare just one entry – a reflective essay that explains how your portfolio represents you as a reader, writer, speaker, listener and viewer.

New Standards English language arts portfolios are designed to be completed at the end of fourth, eighth and tenth grade. The portfolio itself is organized into exhibits. Exhibits have a direct, but not necessarily one-to-one, correspondence to New Standards performance standards for the target grade level. All three grade levels – with one exception – share the same exhibit structure: reading exhibit; writing exhibit; speaking, listening, and viewing exhibit; reflective essay exhibit. Each exhibit consists of several entries. While most entries are actual pieces of student work, some entries will be evaluated by the classroom teacher who will enter a certification that the student has or has not met the standard. For example, at the elementary level, the classroom teacher, using guidelines provided by New Standards, will determine whether a student has or has not achieved fluency in reading aloud. If the teacher judges that the student meets the standard for fluency, he/she will sign a certification of fluency. No additional evidence, such as tape-recordings or written records, is required.

Figure 5.3 below illustrates the design of the middle and high school portfolios. The design is the same for both grade levels.

Figure 5.4 English language arts portfolio field trial middle school sample entry slips

Reading Exhibit   Entry Slip #5

Quantity, Range and Depth in Reading

Attach records and work you've done to show your quantity, range, and depth in reading. For example, attach reading journals, literature logs, book reviews, and response-to-literature papers. Include assignment sheets if you have them.

This entry shows that you've read many different kinds of materials and that you've focused some of your reading on a particular author, genre, issue or topic. People who read your portfolio will look for evidence that you have read:

- At least 25 books or their equivalent in articles, newspapers or textbooks in the course of a year
- Materials that are appropriate for eighth graders and are of high quality (for example, chosen from recognized reading lists
- A well-balanced selection of materials from traditional and contemporary literature and from public discourse
- At least three different kinds – genres – of printed materials (for example, novels, biographies, articles from *Sports Illustrated*, (etc.)
- Works of at least five different writers
- At least four books or book equivalents about one issue or subject, or in one genre, or by a single author

This student has met the standard for quantity, range and depth in reading

Teacher's Name   Teacher's Signature

Reading Exhibit   Entry Slip #2

Reading Accomplishment in Informational Materials

Attach one or two pieces of your writing that demonstrate that you read informational materials well. For example you could attach reports, reading journals, book reviews, and literature logs. Include assignment sheets if you have them.

This entry shows that you can read challenging informational material well. People who read the entry will look for evidence that you can

- Restate from the text by putting what the author said into your own words
- Summarize information
- Relate new information to your own prior knowledge and experience
- Speculate about related topics or information, and/or hypothesize about the information
- Reflect on the information and consider its effectiveness
- Analyze information by drawing inferences, asking questions, or identifying the influence of the author's point of view

Describe the assignment that prompted this work (attach other pages if needed):

What makes this work good evidence for this entry?

Writing Exhibit   Entry Slip #6

A Persuasive Essay

Attach one piece of writing that demonstrates your ability to write persuasively. Include assignment sheets if you have them.

This entry shows your ability to write a persuasive essay. People who read this essay will look for evidence that you can:

- Engage the reader by establishing a context, creating a point of view or persona, and using other appropriate techniques to develop reader interest
- Include a controlling idea that organizes your writing and makes a clear and logical judgment
- Organize your writing in a way that is appropriate to the needs and interests of a specified audience
- Arrange details, reasons, examples, and/or anecdotes effectively and persuasively
- Include appropriate information and arguments; exclude information and arguments that are irrelevant
- Anticipate and address reader concerns and counter-arguments
- Support arguments with detailed evidence, citing sources of information

Describe the assignment that prompted this work (attach other pages if needed);

What makes this work a good piece of evidence for this entry?

Speaking, Listening, and Viewing Exhibit   Entry Slip #4

Speaking Accomplishment: Information

Attach evidence of your ability to make an oral presentation to share information you've gathered. Evidence may include planning notes, an outline, speech notes, or audio or video tapes. In addition, you must include teacher, peer, and self evaluations that demonstrate your ability to do the following:

- Ask appropriate questions
- Respond to the questions of others
- Paraphrase and summarize to increase understanding
- Listen responsively to others' points of view
- Use language that is simple and appropriate for communicating
- Speak audibly

Describe the assignment that prompted this work (attach other pages if needed):

The elementary portfolio differs from the above design in the following ways:

1 Certification of reading fluency is required.
2 Students are not required to show evidence of reading public discourse or functional documents.
3 Only four pieces of writing are required for the writing exhibit.
4 Teacher certification is the only entry required for the speaking, listening, and viewing exhibit.
5 Students write letters of introduction to each exhibit, rather than an essay reflecting on the portfolio as a whole.

Another important feature of the design is that a student may use the same entry more than once. For example, if a student enters a report on the Australian desert in the reading exhibit as evidence of reading accomplishment in informational materials, the student may use the same piece to fulfill the report requirement of the writing exhibit. To do this, the student would simply complete an entry slip referring the reader to the location of the original piece.

Handbooks for each grade level have been created. The handbooks consist primarily of perforated pages of entry slips, which teachers can tear out, duplicate and distribute as needed. Students affix one entry slip to each entry. The entry slip is designed to communicate the criteria for entry selection and scoring, to enable students to articulate their reasons for selection, and to collect information on circumstances of performance. Figure 5.4 displays four sample entry slips. These entry slips were selected to illustrate at least one type of entry for each exhibit (except for the reflective essay exhibit). Note that the entry slip for quantity, range and depth in reading is an example of the 'teacher certification' type entry slip.

During the national portfolio benchmarking meeting in July 1995, participants reviewed several hundred portfolios and selected a set of exemplars at each targeted grade level. The dilemma was that we were looking for portfolios to exemplify the above design, which did not exist when students constructed their portfolios in 1994–1995. Therefore, using a provisional scoring system designed to link the 1994 portfolio design to the 1995 design, we selected benchmark portfolios which could be rearranged and edited to match closely the 1995–96 design. Three exemplars at each grade level (elementary, middle and high school) were sent to partner states and districts for use in training and professional development. At each grade level, two of the portfolios were identified as 'meeting the standards' and one was identified as 'nearing the standards'. Each portfolio was accompanied by an interpretive summary which explained how individual entries and exhibits linked to New Standards performance standards.

Figure 5.5 Portfolio scores (middle and high school design)

Reading exhibit
Reading accomplishment in literature: 1 score
Reading accomplishment in informational materials: 1 score
Teacher certification of quantity, range, depth in reading:
Complete/incomplete

Writing exhibit
Individual writing entries: 1 score each
Holistic evaluation of breadth in writing: 1 score
Conventions (2 entries identified by student): 1 score
Evidence of use of writing processes and strategies: 1 score

Speaking, listening and viewing exhibit
Teacher certification of informal speaking and listening:
Present/not present
Formal speaking and listening: 1 score
Viewing (optional): 1 score

Reflective essay exhibit
Reflective essay: 1 score

Looking inside a New Standards middle school portfolio

Appendix C contains examples of two entries from one middle school port-folio that was identified by participants at the national benchmarking as 'meeting the standards'. These sample entries are reproduced here simply to convey, albeit incompletely, the quality and nature of the work produced by middle school students for the New Standards portfolio. The portfolio from which the samples were chosen contained many other entries which paint a more complete and vivid picture of the student's literacy achieve-ments. The commentary which accompanies the sample entries is intended to link the entry to the criteria given on the entry slip and highlight note-worthy features of the entry.

The current plan for scoring portfolios is designed to yield a score for each exhibit and is displayed in Figure 5.5.

Clearly, many questions remain unanswered about this proposal. For example, it is not yet clear how an exhibit score will be assigned. The criteria for scoring and/or using the reflective essay for scoring have not been set. It is not clear how the 'check' only scores will factor into exhibit scores. Much work needs to be done on criteria for scoring speaking, listening and viewing. Consensus has not been reached on whether there may be interaction among the exhibits. There has been little discussion to date of which scores will be reported to students and how they will be reported. We hope to clarify such issues as these by working closely with participating New Standards teachers as we move into the next stages of our portfolio work.

Some reflections about our portfolio work

We have learned a lot about student assessment and professional development in our portfolio work with New Standards teachers. First, the linking of portfolios and content standards is a tricky business and really operates through several steps and devices:

1   content standards are translated into student performance standards;
2   student performance standards are translated into (or operationalized as) the exercises, tasks and elicited performances listed on the portfolio entry list, including a reflective essay, possibly an interdisciplinary project of some kind, a reading record and so forth; and
3   the student is asked to use entry forms (and the reflective essay) to explain the connections between each entry and one or more student performance standards.

Each entry in the portfolio requires some sort of rationale for its inclusion. For New Standards, it is an entry form on which the student specifies what standard(s) the item represents. The entry forms organize portfolio entries into exhibits of various standards. Thus, entry forms referencing reading accomplishment are grouped together for scoring as an exhibit of that standard. This is not necessarily an easy task. One item (an essay, a video of a speech) can provide evidence on one or more standards, and one curriculum content standard may require as evidence several entries from the portfolio menu. In addition to the reflective essay, the entry form becomes the primary device through which the student structures the portfolio for review by outside reviewers, judges, or auditors. Through the entry form, the student is demonstrating his/her understanding of the relationship among content standards, portfolio contents, and performance standards. Thus, the entry form attached to each portfolio exhibit challenges the student's ability to understand the curriculum content, to translate that content into a performance, and to use the entry form to tie together standards and evidence.

The reflective essay (originally these were introductory letters) of the portfolio also appears to play a critical role. In this letter, the student indicates the special features of the various performances, suggests their connections to standards, and calls attention to exhibits which the student wishes to highlight. To some degree, the teacher and the judge or rater of the portfolio are assessing both the quality of various performances and the reasonableness of entry forms – in other words, the adequacy of the student's logic in connecting performance to standards. Stated another way, portfolio assessment puts the responsibility squarely on the shoulders of the student to explain what he/she is learning – to create a self-portrait through the portfolio. Our experience, thus far, is that judges who face an unstructured, unexplained portfolio face a very difficult, time-consuming task. An adequate judgement requires that the student structure the portfolio for judging. Thus, portfolio assessment is judging not only what students know (declarative knowledge), what they can do (procedural knowledge) and what they can know and do now (conditional knowledge), but also whether students know what they know and can do and whether they can explain their judgement (evaluative knowledge).

For many students, the collection of entries are the default standards, not the performance or content standards which teachers value. For the student, the primary questions are 'What do I put in my portfolio?' and 'How will it be judged?' Our experience is that students at first give only a passing glance toward content standards. For the student, standards only confirm that the portfolio assignments are not the arbitrary decisions of an individual teacher. It is the entry forms and exhibits which encourage students to begin to understand the standards of curriculum content and the way one might organize evidence for standards of performance.

From one point of view, the portfolio becomes a publication in which the reflective essay is the introductory chapter giving the overview. The entry forms specify how each item in the portfolio is to be used for judging. These entries are used to show the standards of depth in reading, breadth in reading, narrative and report writing, and so forth. The exhibits of standards are like chapters in a book. The items or entries are parts of each chapter. In summary, then, the portfolio process tests the way each person – student, teacher and judge – answers the question of whether the item in the portfolio is reasonable evidence of achievement in a content area and whether the performance represents mastery of a given standard. In the process, each stakeholder is learning how the accountability portfolio works as a publication.

The New Standards reference examination

The latest assessment component to be added to the New Standards family of assessments is the reference examination. As we suggested, it consists of multiple-choice and 'short task' components, tasks that can be completed in a single class session. There is not a great deal to say about the format and structure of the examination since it relies heavily on formats with which educators have been familiar for some time.

In its most current iteration, as it is being used in the 1996–97 school year, it consists of three parts. Part 1, which is scheduled for 45 minutes, is a fairly conventional writing to a prompt activity. One example for grade-four students involves describing for a 5-year-old what it was like to be a 5-year-old. A second example, for high school students, involves writing about the ways in which people leave traces of their lives. Across several different forms of the examination, a variety of genres is assessed. This is, of course, consistent with the purpose of the reference exam. Recall that it was spawned in response to criticisms of performance tasks and portfolios and lack of domain coverage was a major criticism.

Part 2, called Reading and Writing, is a mini-version, planned to last 45 minutes, of a multiple-day task such as 'mummies and pyramids'. The questions are open-ended and invite students to engage their personal and critical perspectives. One major difference, imposed by the time constraint, is that the responses are about single rather than multiple texts, inviting a clear intratextual rather than an intertextual stance.

Part 3, the multiple-choice component, is described earlier in this chapter. While we, as active participants in earlier iterations of New Standards assessment development, find little to celebrate in the inclusion of the reference exam, we certainly understand the issues and motives that spawned its development.

As we put the finishing touches on this paper, the reference examination is rapidly becoming the cornerstone of the assessment repertoire of New Standards. Apparently users find that it retains some of the excitement and cutting edge luster of the performance tasks and portfolio activity without attracting the criticisms of expense and psychometric instability that have been levelled at performance examinations in general (e.g., Brennan and Johnson 1995; Mehrens 1992).

This chapter has described the recent experience of teachers and investigators developing and refining alternative assessment tools which document the growth and accomplishment in literacy for both school-based and external constituencies. The authors hope that the account will explain how New Standards is meeting the major challenge: to develop assessment frameworks which maintain a balance between the priorities of the classroom and the imperatives of 'high stakes assessment'.

Conclusion

We learned a great deal in our New Standards work – about the limits and possibilities of assessment, about the nature of staff development to support novel assessments, and about what sustains and what impedes a reform movement.

Regarding assessment, we learned that as a profession we are capable of assuming much more risk than we usually allow ourselves to take. Granted, the teachers who came to work with us in New Standards were hand picked for participation by their state leaders and were dedicated, hard-working teachers who wanted to learn more about the process so that they could do a better job in their own classrooms – which makes them very like most teachers we know and have worked with. What amazed us all, organizers and participants alike, was how much we were capable of learning and doing – and how hard the work was. We also learned that tasks and portfolios engage both teachers and students in the assessment process in very different ways. Assessment is transformed from a 'thing' that gets done to you by some external force into a thing that you (whether 'you' is a teacher or a student) do to yourself. And while that sounds, on the surface at least, like an empowering experience that everyone would want (and many, even most, do), it carries with it some awesome responsibilities – responsibilities that not every student or every teacher is ready for.

We also learned how difficult it is for these new sorts of assessments to measure up to conventional psychometric standards of generalizability. One of the most frustrating aspects of our involvement in New Standards was learning, after all the work and worry we had all invested, that our tasks lacked sufficient interjudge reliability or intertask generalizability. Reliability, conceptualized as stability across judges, situations and tasks, is a hallmark of conventional multiple-choice assessments. Portfolios and performance tasks, on the other hand, gravitate toward difference and uniqueness. In fact, we think a theory of 'difference' along with some strategies for coping with it (see Moss 1994; 1996; Pearson, DeStefano and Garcia, in press), such as moderation and an appeal process, should guide the work of those interested in sustaining performance assessment as a valid educational enterprise.

On the staff development agenda, we also learned much. Most important, assessments that place a premium upon teacher judgement make sense only under the assumption that high levels of professional knowledge – about subject matter, language, culture, and assessment – are widely distributed in the profession. Whenever and wherever the assumption of professional knowledge is suspect, we will have to invest in staff development. School systems must either decide to make this investment or resort to tests that require little or no interpretation.

Our experience with teachers in New Standards underscores the importance of teacher knowledge and the construct of a community of professional judgement. We found that at every stage along the way – from task development, to implementation, to scoring – the key element in whatever success we experienced was bringing teachers together to examine and to wrestle with, both collaboratively and dialectically, the question of what counts as evidence of quality in student work. This was obvious to the teachers in their evaluations of the conferences, and it was equally as apparent to those of us who organized the events. When asked why such experiences have proven valuable, the New Standards teachers told us that in the process of figuring out how to elicit good work, as well as in the process of judging the quality of student work, they are forced to consider a range of important professional concerns and bodies of knowledge such as the language arts curriculum (and the opportunities it provides or ignores), the language and cultural perspectives that students bring to their learning, and issues in assessment itself. Thus, while the challenge of professional development is daunting, the fact that the process of task development and implementation carries with it such enormous intellectual energy should give us hope that we can meet the challenge.

We also learned a lot about sustaining a reform effort. New Standards was, and to a degree still is, nothing short of an attempt to reform the instructional landscape of schools in the United States. Ironically, the lessons we learned on this front come more from our frustrations than our successes. New Standards was based upon the premise that assessments, because of their high stakes role in programme accountability, have played such an important role in thwarting attempts to establish new and challenging curricula. New and different assessments must play a similarly important role in leading the way to a better curricular world for students and teachers. What we learned, we think, is that there is no substitute for a good curriculum and that the assessment has yet to be built that can stand as a surrogate for curriculum. Even the best and noblest of assessments is not up to the challenge, and they can be compromised when the stakes get too high. So the only safeguard for students and teachers is to lead with curriculum – to establish the goals and standards that frame a challenging curriculum. Then, and only then, comes the appropriate role for assessment – to sustain the efforts of teachers and students in meeting those goals and standards. We could ask for no better role for assessment within language arts.

References

Brennan, R.L. and Johnson, E.G. (1995) 'Generalizability of performance assessments' *Educational Measurement: Issues and Practices*, 14 (4), 9–12, 27.

Mehrens, W.A. (1992) 'Using performance assessment for accountability purposes' *Educational Measurement: Issues and Practices*, 11 (3), 3–9, 20.

Moss, P. (1994) 'Can there be validity without reliability?' *Educational Researcher*, 23 (2), 5–12.

Moss, P. (1996) 'Enlarging the dialogue in educational measurement: Voices from interpretive research traditions' *Educational Researcher*, 25 (1), 20–28.

New Standards (1993) Holistic reading rubric – July 1993. Rochester, NY: New Standards.

New Standards (1994) Task development packet – July 1994. Rochester, NY: New Standards.

Pearson, P.D., DeStefano, L. and García, G.E. (in press) 'Dilemmas in reading assessment' To appear in C. Harrison and T. Salinger (Eds.), *Assessing Reading 1: Theory and Practice*, London: Routledge.

Resnick, L.B. and Resnick, D.P. (1992) 'Assessing the thinking curriculum: New tools for educational reform' In B.R. Gifford and M.C. O'Connor (eds.) *Changing assessments: Alternative views of aptitude, achievement, and instruction*. (pp. 37–75). Boston: Kluwer Academic Publishers.

Shepard, Lorrie A. (1993) 'The place of testing reform in educational reform: a reply to Cizek' *Educational Researcher*, 22 (4), 10–13.

Spalding, E. (1995a) 'Teachers' views of New Standards English language arts performance assessment tasks', paper presented at the National Reading Conference, New Orleans, November, 1995.

Spalding, E. (1995b) 'The New Standards Project and English Language Arts portfolios: A report on process and progress' *The Clearing House*, 68 (4), 219–224.

Wiggins, G. (1993) *Assessing student performance: Exploring the purpose and limits of testing*, San Francisco, CA: Jossey-Bass.

Appendix A: Sample reading response and commentary

Mummies and Pyramids Reading Response: Score Point 4

1 From what you have read and seen, discuss the purpose of Egyptian pyramid building. Include in your discussion at least two factors which made this achievement possible.

Egypt's pyramids are the oldest stone buildings in the world. Inside their once-smooth white limestone surfaces, there are secret passageways, hidden rooms, ramps, bridges, shafts. Pyramids were not built for exploring. They served for reflective reasons. Ancient Egyptians had a strong belief in life after death. The Kings, called Pharoahs wanted their bodies to last forever, so they built pyramids to protect a pharoah's preserved body. It also had the goods he would need in the next life to continue living as he had when he was alive.

Ancient Egypt had a unique combination of ingredients for building pyramids. To build the pyramids, great supplies of raw materials were needed. Two kinds of rocks were quarried close to the banks of the Nile River. They were transported on the Nile in wooden boats. This circle of isolation allowed the Egyptians to work in peace and security.

Commentary on Response

In this response, the reader has para-phrased selectively information drawn from two articles in the *Kids Discover Pyramids* magazine. From these articles, the reader has synthesized information in order to completely, succinctly and accurately discuss the purpose of the pyramids and two factors (raw materials and isolation) which made the achieve-ment possible. The response demonstrates both a thorough under-standing and an interpretation (Pyramids 'served for reflective reasons') of the texts read.

2   What have you learned about life in ancient Egypt from the objects found in the tombs? Give examples to support what you say.

Mummies tell us a lot about Ancient Egypt. One of the main things which were found in tombs had to do with their religion. Ancient Egyptians believed that everlasting life took place in a paradise known as the 'Field of Reeds'. To get there, the dead had to pass through an underworld filled with fearsome monsters. To help insure a safe passage, they were given a spell book. A copy was placed in each tomb. If you were evil like Ginger you were buried with knives and pots. If you were well liked you were given jewels, furniture, the animal mummy such as a cat, dog, or crocodile etc. . . . If you were close to someone like King Tut was placed in his tomb as his stillborn daughter's mummies, and a lock of hair from his grandmother Queen Tiya.

The reader continues to paraphrase selectively and synthesize information from several articles in the magazine. The reader has chosen to focus on religion in this response. Here the reader advances an original interpretation, making a connection between people's goodness (rather than wealth) in this life, and the worth of objects entombed with them. (Note: Ginger is the name given by archaeologists to one of the mummies mentioned in the readings.)

Commentary on Response

The reader succinctly states the purpose of mummification, then carefully describes the process. In the second part of the response, the reader makes connections to personal knowledge of modern funerary practices in order to construct a point-by-point contrast to the first part of the response.

3 Compare and contrast the ancient Egyptians' reason for mummification with what you know of modern peoples' practices regarding death.

The Egyptians believed that life after death was very similar to life on earth. Their dead, therefore, had to be protected and preserved for the next life. To preserve the body, a process known as mummification was developed around 2600 BC. Mummification might take as long as 70 days. First they would take out the brains through the nostrils. Then the vital organs were taken out and put into jars. The body was dried out for 40 days. The body is then embalmed. The body was then wrapped in linen bandages. Priest and embalmers performed ritual gestures at every step in the mummification process.

Today in the 90's its a little bit different. We don't believe there's life after death. To preserve the bodies these days it only takes a few hours. We keep all the organs inside. We just drain all the fluids out. We then put embalming fluid in the veins. Then there is a choice you cremate the body, or buried it underground. Then there is a funeral and a religious ceremony.

Here, the reader makes strong connections between information gained from reading and prior knowledge. In this response, the reader skilfully alternates between accounts of Egyptian and modern building techniques.

---

4   If the pyramids were built today, how would the process be different from the process described in Kids Discover magazine? Who would be involved in the building and what tools and materials would be used? Is there anything else that would be different? Why?

The process would be different first of all because in the 90's we would have a blue print of what we are building. Building pyramids are difficult and dangerous to build. It requires a highly organized society to do it. Today we would not build it out of limestone and granite. We would build it out of glass, stone, or brick. And most have four sloping sides that meet at a point. The people involved in building the pyramid today would be highly skilled carpenters, and construction workers. Today's tools are made of steel. The ancient Egyptians used tools of copper, a softer metal than steel. Today we use cranes, bulldozers, hammers, cement, plastic etc. as tools. It would take us more than 2 years to finish building the pyramid.

Commentary on Response

This lengthy letter to Dr Carter gives extensive evidence of this reader's ability to make personal connections to texts. The reader follows each 'chunk' of information with a personal evaluation (e.g., 'I think that's an odd way to get a name for a mummy'). The reader also makes connections to and evaluates information in terms of the larger community of potential readers of Dr Carter's book (e.g., 'Some children like to read about gory things').

This reader does not simply present information, but tests it against personal experience and reflects on how others might react (e.g. 'I don't think I would like these items inside my dead body. . . . I don't know if people would like items inside their dead bodies'). Sometimes the reader's

---

WRITE A REVISED DRAFT

Now you will write a revised draft. Use the ideas you got from your classmate to improve your letter. Remember, you do not have to use all of the ideas, only the ones that you think will improve your letter. Write your revised draft in the space below.

Dear Dr. Mary Carter,

Hello! My name is _____. I have some fascinating inforemation, facts and suggestions to put in your young adult book about Mummies. I think you should start with how mummies got their name. Mummies got their name from the Arabic name 'mummiya' meaning Bitumen-beetle. This is because the resin with which some mummies were filled turned them black over the centuries until they looked like a beetle. I think that's an odd way to get a name for a mummy.

Egyptians believed that life after death to them was similar to life on earth. To me it is very fascinating they believed life after death was simlar to life on earth.

insights are surprising and original (e.g., 'Children would think that it is hilarious to have a bug inside your body').

This reader has used multiple text sources efficiently and appropriately, synthesizing information from several different articles in the *Kids Discover* magazine and the task *Reader*.

Their dead, therefore, had to be protected and preserved for the next life. To preserve the body, a drying out process known as mummification was developed around 2600 B.C. Mummification might take as long as 70 days. First they pull the brain through the nostrils. Then the dead person's internal organs were removed and stored in special vases. The body was dried out for 40 days. Some children like to read about gory things. A carved scarab was put in place of the heart. Magical writing on the scarab was supposed to keep the heart from speaking out and perhaps giving a bad impression of its owner during the heart and feather trial. Children would think it is hilarious to have a bug inside your body.

The body was then dried out with nitrogen salt, then sometimes packed with spices, sawdust, straw, and a kind of glassy black stuf called Bitumen. Which hardens until it was like cememt. I don't think I would like those items inside my dead body. It would make me look overweight in my afterlife. I just wouldn't want my appearance to look that way. I don't know if people would like items inside their dead bodies.

Egyptians mummified animals like their pets. Just to see them in the afterworld. They also mummified sacred animals such as crocodiles, jackels and baboons, those associated with Egyptian gods & goddesses. I agree with the Egyptians I would bury my dog _____ with me to see her in my afterlife. I think people would agree with me, pets are like people so you would have them buried with you.

Ancient Egyptians believed that everlasting life took place in a paradise known as the Field of Reeds. To get there, the dead had to pass through a underworld filled with fearsome monsters, and demons. To get there safely, the priest put together a collection of spells. A copy was placed in each tomb. I think it would be interesting to travel while your dead through an underworld. Along with a collection of spells to go through safely. Children would think its like reading a fantasy story.

About 1,350 B.C. a young boy 9 years old, named Tutankamen (Tut for short) became King. He died at the age of 18. King Tut was buried inside 4 coffins made of pure gold. Inside the chambers their are chariots, jewels, gold masks, a golden throne, etc . . . Things he needed in his afterlife. I think a lot of young people would like to have the experience of being a King at such a young age.

Mummies were layed to rest in pyramids. Ancient Egyptians had a strong belief in life after death. The Kings, called Pharoah's wanted their bodies to last forever, so they had pyramids built to protect their bodies after death. Each pyramid housed a pharoah's preserved body. I think I would have wanted my body to be layed for my after life in a pyramid. Young people will think its interesting to be buried in a pyramid.

I hope the information I gave you will help you write an excellent book about Mummies. I think young people will enjoy the inforemation. Good luck! writing the book.

Sincerely

Commentary on Response

Summary

This is a score point 4 paper because it demonstrates thoughtful and purposeful reading. The reader has exhibited thorough understanding of whole texts, synthesized information from several texts, developed plausible interpretations of texts, made connections to personal experience and prior knowledge throughout the response and, as appropriate, reflected on the meaning and implications of information read. Although this reader takes few risks, it should be remembered that this informational task does not offer explicit opportunities for challenging the authors or the texts.

Appendix B: Sample writing response and commentary

Mummies and Pyramids Writing Response: Score Point 4

Dr Mary Carter is an archeologist who is studying how the ancient pyramids of Egypt were built. She is considering hiring a few young people to travel with her team and help with the work. Write her a persuasive letter which will convince her that your knowledge of pyramids makes you a person she should hire. Give details and be specific.

Dear Dr. Carter

Hello. I am an 8th grader at ___ Middle School. I would like to be one of the young people who you take with you on your pyramid excavations. I believe that I am well qualified, and I hope you will think that way when you have finished with this letter.

Since I received notice of your intentions, I have been doing some background reading on pyramids. I have learned some interesting and/or new facts, some that others may not know. One of the most interesting facts I discovered had to do with the construction of the pyramids. I had known that the pyramid base was perfectly level, but I just couldn't figure out how the Egyptians had done it. Then I read a *Discover Magazine*

Commentary on Response

The writer clearly states the purpose and adopts a stance appropriate for the task – to convince Dr Carter to accept his or her credentials. The writer maintains this courteous yet authoritative tone throughout.

The writer contextualizes the task by referring to the fact that 'I have been doing some background reading'. The writer also cites sources of information.

The writer's voice emerges through such personal comments as, '. . . I just couldn't figure out how the Egyptians had done it.'

Each paragraph explores a key idea, e.g. how pyramid bases were levelled. The writer elaborates on the idea with information synthesized from text sources. The information reported is accurate. The writer keeps the reader engaged by concluding each paragraph on pyramids followed by a reader on the same subject. Through the magazine I learned that they built troughs to hold water along the pyramid's base. The Egyptians filled them, and where the waterline was uneven, so was the base. I was amazed at the ingenuity of the ancient Egyptians. They made a simple solution for an arduous problem.

A second fact I learned from the magazine was also about the construction. I learned that pyramids had air shafts dug in them so that the people could breath during the funeral service. These were built by making holes in each layer of the pyramid as it was being erected. I found this interesting because it was an example of Egyptian problem solving. Although a clever idea, I wonder how many people suffocated before the engineers and architects figured it out.

Another fact I learned was the time involved after finding artifacts in a pyramid. The cataloging of King Tut's pyramid took over 10 years for around 3000 objects. And this was only a few rooms of a relatively unimportant pharoah's tomb. Just think if Khufu's Great Pyramid, the only one of the 7 wonders of the world still standing, had not been raided, how long it would take to catalog that.

---

with a personal observation.

Transitions between paragraphs are clear. The progression of ideas is logical, beginning with general facts about pyramid construction, moving to discussion of specific pyramids and their reasons for their construction. The final reason the writer gives for wanting to join the expedition – the fact that 'only 80 pyramids [are] still standing today' – brings appropriate closure to the letter.

Throughout the letter, the writer supports ideas effectively through such strategies as explaining the pyramids' significance ('This is why pyramids were built so that the pharoah's body would have a resting spot . . .'); making inferences (e.g. 'Although a clever idea, I wonder how many people suffocated . . .'); and drawing conclusions (e.g. 'They made a simple solution for an arduous problem').

Commentary on Response

The writer's word choices are sophisticated and precise (e.g. 'ingenuity', 'arduous', 'relatively important'). Likewise, sentence structures are complex and varied.

Mechanical errors are few, given the length and complexity of the piece. Throughout, the writer adheres to the conventions of formal letter-writing.

Summary

This piece of writing maintains focus and coherence, while keeping the reader engaged with its courteous yet personal tone. The writer states ideas clearly and supports them with accurate information. This writer has demonstrated a clear command of vocabulary, sentence structure and writing conventions.

One of the most interesting facts I learned had to do with the reasoning behind the building of the pyramids and some Egyptian philosophy. Ancient Egyptians believed that their pharoah was the man-child of the Sun God, and when he died, he went to live with the Sun God in the west. This is why the pyramids were built, so that the pharoah's body would have a resting spot while the spirit went west, which is why the pyramids were always built on the west bank of the Nile.

The final reason I have for wanting to be taken on this expedition is that there are only 80 pyramids still standing today. With this limited number, I want to learn as much as possible about ancient Egyptians, and I believe the pyramids hold the answers. Thank you for your time.

Appendix C: Sample entries from middle school English language arts portfolio

Entry for Reading Accomplishment in Literature

Criteria from the Entry Slip:

- **Develop and explore concepts, issues and themes in texts**
- **Analyze, interpret, and evaluate a text and/or parts of a text (for example, chapters, stanzas, acts)**
- **Identify and discuss elements of the author's craft, including word choice, author's purpose, text structure and text function**
- **Relate literary material you read to cultural and/or political issues**
- **Make connections:**
  - **among parts of a text (for example, chapter to chapter, beginning to end)**
  - **among several texts you've read**
  - **between texts and your own experience**
- **Challenge or question texts (for example, question an author's logic, speculate about an author's biases)**

Commentary on Response

The opening paragraph of this book report shows the student's ability to evaluate a text ('I thought it was a babyish children's book...') and to revise that evaluation upon reflection ('The book... was actually very wonderful').

After giving a brief summary of the whole book, the student begins a detailed analysis of one story, 'The Bridge Builder'. As might be expected in a book report, the student first summarizes the plot before analysing its meaning. In this portion of the report, the student demonstrates the ability to generate and explore themes in the text (e.g. 'Bridges are needed in unexpected places just for the reason that they're there', and 'Are we all

The Door in the Air and Other Stories

When my mom brought home a book she had gotten from the library for me, I thought it was a babyish children's book since it was short. The book, called The Door in the Air, by Margaret Mahy, was actually very wonderful, and I'm glad I read it. The stories were so true and beautiful, that the book was like a treasure.

The Door in the Air was a book composed of nine different tales of fantasy about wizards, castles, bridges, changes, and life. The way they were written gave each story an aura of truth. Each story told a meaning of life. One tale, The Two Sisters, told how two twin daughters were exact opposites. One was of light, the other darkness. But by the end, each daughter gave their ill mother an important gift. Another story was about two people who finally let themselves go to the wind. The Door in the Air taught about art, unexpectedness and changes of the world.

One of the best stories in the book was called The Bridge Builder. It was about this traveler named Merlin who had a father who worked as a bridge builder. At first, to buy his children's christmas presents,

the same people as we walk through time? is what I ask.') Recognition of the symbolism of bridges is implicit in statements such as these.

The student personally connects with the text: 'I believe in the principle of Merlin's father.' The student shows appreciation of the author's craft with such statements as, '[The bridge] was made of silver thread and mother of pearl and was to be crossed at midnight.' Finally, the student aptly summarizes her interpretation of the story's major theme: 'The tale is about life – seasons, seconds; passing and changing.'

Commentary on Response

Here the student uses anecdote to reveal strong personal connections to the text – so strong that she shares this favourite story with her father by reading it aloud to him. Statements such as '. . . I read, with much feeling as I really loved the story', are indications of this reader's interpretive ability. Her engagement with the text can be inferred from her meticulous account of every single interruption to her reading of her favourite story. This reader understands that reading is a social act, and acknowledges the risks inherent in sharing texts with others: 'I was a little disappointed in that. I always expect better reactions from people, but he seemed not to think the story as important as I believed.'

---

he built practical bridges where people told him to build them. But after his children grew up, he built bridges of his dreams, that were artistic masterpieces. The bridges were in unusual places, one was over a volcano with harps and handrails, some were in forests over rivers, some contained beautiful caged birds and fish. There were hanging garden bridges and bridges built on the city on top of skyscrapers. But since people could not cross all the bridges or even cross them in the same way, the government was angry and soldiers were sent out to get Merlin's father. When they came to a forest, Merlin said a magic word, half made up, and his father turned into a bridge the helped the soldiers who were falling in the river. I thought that story was so beautiful. I believe in the principles of Merlin's father. Bridges are needed in unexpected places just for the reason that they are there. You can know a bridge is out there somewhere in the world and never find it. Or maybe it will just crumble. But it was there. The world is full of wonder, and Merlin's father made odd bridges that suspended over rivers and add surprise to life.

Merlin's father questioned if a man would be the same man he was before he crossed a bridge. Are we all the same people as we walk

Entry for Reading Accomplishment in Literature

Summary

Only an excerpt of this entry is reprinted here. In succeeding paragraphs, this student continues to demonstrate the interpretive skills and aesthetic stance of an accomplished reader of literature.

through time? is what I ask. I also loved the idea of a bridge Merlin's father made. It was made of silver thread and mother of pearl and was to be crossed at midnight. When you crossed it you would walk into the next day. This story told that by strolling across the bridges of the world, you would change somehow. The tale is about life – seasons, seconds, passing and changing.

I liked the story so much that I decided to tell it to my dad. It was a hot afternoon and I brought the straw mat out to sit on, and two books: *The Door in the Air* and another one called *California Blue*. My dad was outside too, cleaning something. I decided to read my favorite tale, *The Bridge Builder*, for him. As he cleaned, I read, with much feeling as I really loved the story. I paused every few minutes to ask if he was listening, and repeated a few parts as necessary. Twice my dad went inside the house to get some things. On the later trip, he brought back slices of watermelon. Then, my cat Silver jumped over the fence and rested himself in front of us. He looked so funny because he was laying on his stomach with his legs stretched out in back of him, and his eyes were mischievous as they always get when he goes outside. My dad spit watermelon seeds on Silver to annoy him, and Silver just lay there, contented, with dark brown seeds on his back. We were interupted four times when an employee of my mom's came in and when a guy opened the fence to ask if we wanted our lawn mowed (we didn't). Then my mom asked me if I wanted some mashed potatoes with gravy and I said yes. She stuck a large bowl of the white and brown snack through the window to me. My dad also interupted to explain a part on why words were magic. Olden day magicians would know the essence of a word, and when they said it right, it would make things happen. Every time I was fin-ished, my dad told me he thought it was good. He read some parts to himself, and he said the story rang true. I was a little disappointed in that. I always expect better reactions from people, but he seemed not to think the story as important and beautiful as I believed.

Entry for Writing Accomplishment: Writing in a Literary Genre

Criteria from the Entry Slip:
- **Use organizational patterns, formats, language, and other conventions appropriate for the genre you've selected.**
- **Effectively control the genre's techniques.**

Student's description of the assignment:

Everyone in my creative writing class had to write a poem that told what it's not telling. I didn't exactly grasp the concept, but I still like the poem. I wrote it out of my own experience when I was dancing outside with the wind. I like the poem.

> Cat
>
> It is not me – dancing
> with the wind, crashing
> out the door with the
> wind blowing my hair
> to the sky.
>
> It is not me –
> reaching my hands toward
> the wildly rocking trees

Commentary on Response

This free verse poem shows that this student uses effectively the organizational patterns, language and other conventions appropriate to this form of poetry. First the poem displays a deliberate pattern of organization both within stanzas and across stanzas. The writer successfully creates and maintains a mysterious tone. Effective visual images are used throughout the poem – 'wind blowing my hair to the sky', 'the wildly rocking trees', 'with a jump over the fence and a spark in his eyes'. Words and phrases throughout the poem mimic the sound of wind (e.g. 'untamed blowing and moaning'). The repeated use of the sound 'w' enhances the auditory impact of the poem. The writer has handled poetic language with skill and sensitivity.

with a song in my head
and a step to my feet.

No, it is not me – dancing and leaping
to the untamed blowing and moaning –

But my cat. With a jump
over the fence and a spark
in his eyes, bewildered
at the crazy girl who is
dancing with the wind.

Part II

LINKING CURRICULUM
AND ASSESSMENT
IN THE CLASSROOM

6

RESPONSIVE ASSESSMENT OF READING

Seeking evidence on reading attainment from students

Colin Harrison, Mary Bailey and Chris Foster

In this chapter, we attempt to examine the potential of some often-neglected approaches to the problem of seeking evidence of reading achievement, by reporting case studies based on interviews, book reports on leisure reading, and tape-recordings made by students. We do not begin with the case studies, however, important though these are. We begin by asking a prior question, which we think is also often neglected. This is the crucial question of the basis on which we should consider innovation or change in assessment, and what we suggest is that there are some first principles upon which we can build, and which lead us to put forward the notion of *responsive assessment*, some aspects of which we try to illustrate in the case studies.

In the next section of this chapter, we review the six principles of what we term 'responsive assessment', which have been more fully explained in our chapter in the companion volume to this one (Harrison, Bailey and Dewar 1998). We go on to reiterate some points made in that chapter about the elusiveness of reading processes. These discussions lead to the suggestion that evidence gathered directly from students can be of value in reading assessment and that it may be used for a variety of purposes. The remainder of this chapter then goes on to examine some examples of such evidence and to consider some of the ways in which it may be used.

In using the term 'responsive assessment', by the way, we acknowledge our debt to the seminal work of Robert Stake on responsive evaluation (Stake 1979). We also would wish to recognize the important contribution of McGregor and Meirs (1991), who used the term 'responsive evaluation' in their work in Australia on assessment in language and reading.

Six principles of responsive assessment

In our chapter in the book which is a companion volume to this one, *Assessing Reading: Theory and Practice*, we identified what we termed 'six postmodern perspectives' which led to some broad principles which we felt should underpin reading assessment. The six principles, underpinning what we have called responsive assessment, were as follows:

1   In responsive assessment, the focus must be on the classroom. Assessment is often a national project and national initiatives may be driven by political imperatives rather than informed by theories of teaching or learning. One key insight of a postmodern perspective is that large-scale 'global' solutions to problems are no longer likely to be regarded as valid and that smaller-scale 'local' solutions may come to be regarded as more useful. When applied in the field of reading assessment, we would argue that this should lead to our focusing attention on the classroom as the site for exploration and analysis, rather than the school or school system. This change of emphasis away from the school or the nation as the unit of assessment turns the spotlight away from a potentially fruitless search for norm-referenced statistics and instead puts a new emphasis on curriculum practices and the place of assessment within teaching and learning. At this point assessment can begin to serve two essential purposes which national programmes usually ignore: assessment evidence can be of direct value to the teacher and it can be of direct value to the student. This is a fundamental reconceptualization of the nature of reading assessment, but we would argue that it must be the starting point for a system of assessing reading whose intention is to raise achievement, rather than simply to report achievement.

2   Responsive assessment calls for an increased emphasis on teacher assessment, peer assessment and self-assessment. Postmodern accounts of scientific enquiry are very sceptical towards claims of 'objectivity' in science and argue that it is important to accept that subjectivity permeates all human enquiry, including science. A postmodern perspective, therefore, seeks to acknowledge the importance of the individual subject. We would want to apply this argument to reading assessment by suggesting that it is essential to put a fresh emphasis on the importance of the teacher and the learner as subjects rather than objects within the assessment process. There is a danger that the teacher can be deskilled by assessment practices which view the teacher simply as a technician who administers tests and whose subjectivity is perceived as a threat to the validity of the assessment process. Instead, we would support the view advanced by the Scottish contributors to this book, Louise Hayward and Ernie Spencer, that teachers are crucial potential

contributors to assessment, but contributors who need professional support to become more skilled and more confident in this complex field. Equally, we would want to argue that an emphasis on the individual subject implies that students themselves should be helped to become confident and skilled in self- and peer-assessment processes.

3 Responsive assessment of reading should not only draw upon a range of methodologies, but should also be negotiated with the participants. Postmodern theories of scientific enquiry have recognized that it is currently no longer possible to describe the world of science with a single theory. Within the world of science, different theories and discourses have to be used under different circumstances. Similar challenges have faced those working in research in the social sciences, as traditional research approaches have been challenged and ethnographers and others have developed new techniques of carrying out research. We would want to advance a similar argument in the field of reading and to suggest that in reading assessment it is important to consider a range of methodologies, and to match these to the needs of different audiences and contexts. In our view, to do this in a manner which recognizes the importance of the individual subject would involve not only using a range of methodologies and approaches, but also negotiating these with the participants. We would want to suggest, for example, that students should be involved in deciding what evidence of their response to reading is to be recorded, and that the range of evidence should be broadened to include material as rich and varied as the following: play scripts, logs, scrapbooks, narratives, maps, graphs, taped conversations, photographs, role-playing, interviews and displays.

4 We would argue that it is important to increase the authenticity of the tasks which form the basis of reading assessment. Postmodern perspectives within literary theory have been very influential in introducing a mistrust of authoritarian notions of meaning in text, and in giving increased importance to the role of the reader in determining a text's meaning. Such a perspective would lead us to challenge some traditional approaches of assessing response to reading, for example, through the use of reading comprehension tests. One aspect of rethinking traditional approaches to reading assessment, therefore, has been to put greater emphasis on considering readers' responses to authentic reading tasks in more naturalistic contexts.

5 It is important to take greater account of a reader's response. Just as important as increasing the authenticity of tasks, in our view, is the need to attempt to capture the authenticity of response to reading which takes place within a task, and to obtain evidence of the transactions which form the reader's response. In looking for ways to take account of this perspective in reading assessment, we suggest that interviews can offer a basis for exploration which is potentially very fruitful.

JOHN RYLANDS
UNIVERSITY
LIBRARY OF
MANCHESTER

There are a number of reasons why we feel that interviews can be especially useful for retaining a variety of types of information on reader response: interviews can be open-ended and dynamic; taped data can be stored, retained and played back later for comparison and discussion; unlike many other ways we use to gain evidence of response to reading, tape-recording does not require the student to have to write; tape-recording also offers the potential for a teacherless context for collecting evidence, over which a student or group of students can have some authority and sense of ownership.

6   Responsive assessment of reading should acknowledge a diminution of the authority of the author and of the text. As Terry Eagleton has pointed out (1983: 74) literary theorists have shifted their attention away from the author and the text and towards the reader, who has hitherto been the most underprivileged of the three. Current theories place the reader at the centre of meaning-making, and view readers as active collaborators in a dynamic process in which predictions, assumptions and inferences are made, challenged and rejected, as the readers gain new insights not only into texts, but also into themselves. In our view, tasks which involve the reader in active reflection on texts, with the active hypothesis formation, dialogue and engagement which are possible in small group work, offer great potential for achieving this final goal, which positions the reader in a central and powerful role as an active and purposeful user of texts and creator of meaning.

We feel that it is important to restate these principles at the outset, because they form the framework for what follows in this chapter.

The elusiveness of reading processes

It is much more difficult than has been often recognized to capture a person's response to reading. The fact that so much work has been carried out over the past fifty years on reading assessment can at least partially blind us to the fact that it is extraordinarily difficult to get at what happens when a person is reading. We often talk about 'comprehension' as if the term can be used with precision to describe a person's knowledge state, but in reality this is rarely the case. A more radical view, but one whose implications we feel it is important to consider, is the following: that there is no such thing as 'reading comprehension', at least not in the way we have traditionally used the term.

We would want to argue that just as the reading processes which occur at or around the moment of word recognition are currently best regarded as dynamic and interactive, so the reading comprehension processes which begin at the point of word recognition (but which also continue during and after reading, as information is reflected on and integrated into long-term memory) should also be viewed as dynamic and flexible. We know that during normal reading a reader's eye makes about four fixations per second, and current theories suggest that most comprehension monitoring occurs automatically and concurrently as the brain decides where the eye will make its next fixation to collect information from the text. On this interpretation, comprehension is an activity, not a fixed knowledge state. As we argued in our chapter in *Assessing Reading 1: Theory and Practice*, a reader understands a text not so much in the manner of 'understanding' the significance of an exit sign, but more in the manner of understanding *The Times Concise Atlas of the World*, or as one understands New York City. In other words, comprehension is dynamic, fluid, socially and culturally located, and acquires temporary stability only in goal-related and purposive contexts, which may have little to do with the understandings which are generated in other contexts.

Given that this is the case, we suggest three points that need to be borne in mind when considering the problem of attempting to collect information about reading and reading processes:

- We need to be aware of the fluidity and inaccessibility of reading processes.
- We need to be aware of the inevitable intrusiveness of assessment in relation to reading and the reading process, and that any method of evoking or making assessable a reader's response is likely to change that response, in cognitive but also in affective dimensions.
- We need to be aware that responding in writing to what has been read requires a double transformation, from reading response into verbal discourse and then into written form, and in the light of this we should consider methods of eliciting responses to reading which do not disadvantage those who are not fluent writers.

These points highlight some of the pedagogic and cognitive challenges we face when we seek to collect information on response to reading. Clearly there are also other perspectives which deserve consideration, not least those related to the social context of assessment practices. Peter Johnston's (1993) work on assessment as social practice reminds us of some of these issues. It is important to acknowledge that both schooling in general and assessment in particular have roles in our society which are to do with power, authority and socialization. This being the case, it would be naïve to fail to acknowledge that in conducting interviews, for example, what is being collected are data which belong to a discourse of schooling and which are not independent of that bounded social milieu. Interviews, book reports and tape-recordings may capture some of the immediacy of a reader's interaction with a text, but they may also permit the rehearsal of a view which the student believes the teacher wants to hear. Such a possibility does not invalidate the use of this type of evidence, but it does remind us of the need to be aware that the discourse is collected in a particular social context, and that the context will be constraining and will determine the nature of the discourse in unavoidable ways.

Assessment at the national level

Upon what basis should a nation's approach to assessment be decided? What we want to argue is that the most useful and worthwhile approaches to reading assessment should be formative and should have four stages:

1 Stage one would be to determine a set of cognitive and pedagogic principles to underpin assessment in general;
2 Stage two would be to apply the principles identified in stage one to the best model of reading development currently available to us;
3 Stage three would be to make principled connections between the model of reading development identified in stage two and the achievements of students;
4 Stage four would be to clarify how curriculum and instruction might be used to accelerate a student's progress beyond the point currently reached, as decided in stage three.

In our model, the four stages are intimately related. However, a government may develop an approach to assessment which ignores the potential interrelationship between the stages altogether. This point is made more clearly if we reformulate the four stages as a series of questions:

1 What approach should be taken to assessment?
2 What should be assessed?
3 How should the assessment be conducted?
4 What should be done with the assessment data?

In England and Wales, one could argue that during the period 1988–94 the UK government's answers to questions 3) and 4), which were that assessment should be conducted using short, pencil and paper tests, and that the assessment data should be used to construct national tables of school performance (Clarke 1990), set an impossible agenda for the test construction agencies which took on the thankless task of writing the test papers. Ostensibly, the tests were required to determine which of ten (subsequently reduced to eight) levels of achievement a student had reached, but an unwillingness to permit the test developers to address questions 1) and 2) did much to help bring about the national test boycott, and to convince teachers and many parents that the £35,000,000 spent on the test development was a waste of money (LATE 1995). Indeed, most testing experts, including those commissioned by the government's testing agency, came to the conclusion that the tests were too narrow to be formative and too unreliable to be summative (see, for example, Ruddock, Brooks, Harris, Salt, Putman and Schagen 1995).

In the period following the 1993 boycott, there have been many signs that the government's testing agency, the Schools Curriculum and Assessment Authority (SCAA), has been moving towards a more flexible approach to testing and towards curriculum specification, but one enduring problem has remained. This is the insistence on requiring teachers and tests to place all students in the age range 7–14 years on one of eight global levels of attainment in English. The difficulty faced by both teachers and test constructors is evident when one considers the following, which is the text of one of the Attainment Target descriptions for Reading (DFE 1995: 28): 'In responding to a range of texts, pupils show understanding of significant ideas, themes, events and characters, beginning to use inference and deduction. They refer to text when explaining their views. They locate and use ideas and information' (level 4).

Not surprisingly, both teachers and assessment specialists have found it difficult to apply level descriptions such as these in making assessments of children's achievement in reading. This is an important point for teachers all over the English-speaking world, since statements such as these are being written by members of committees with an interest in the reading curriculum, all of whom are keen to raise standards, but many of whom know little about reading assessment. There seems to be general agreement that these level descriptions (in the USA they might be called 'standards') offer a helpful and concise reminder of key skill areas which merit attention within the reading curriculum, but many assessment specialists feel that such descriptions are unworkable as a basis for determining the level of an individual's or a nation's reading attainment.

Level descriptions or 'standards' such as those quoted above are not the only basis on which the assessment of reading can locate its foundations, however. The data which we report in the remainder of this chapter represent an attempt by teachers to start, not with attainment levels, but at the other end of the assessment process, with the voices of children, as they talk about what they read, how they read, and how they see themselves as readers. We want to argue that such an approach is not only of greater potential benefit to the student, it can be very useful for the teacher. We also want to go further and to argue that by using different kinds of information, teachers can bring together evidence which meets the six principles of assessment outlined above, and which can also go a long way towards overcoming some of the problems associated with the inaccessibility of the reading process. In our view, such data can be used to contribute to both formative and summative accounts of reading attainment. We want to argue that, working within classrooms, teachers and students can produce evidence which is valid and reliable, evidence which gains its validity through the use of authentic contexts for collecting information and its reliability through the use of cumulative information, collected over time. Our case studies cover only part of the picture, but we would suggest that they are moving us in a more hopeful direction than that taken by approaches to assessment which begin in government offices, rather than the classroom.

Case study 1: The reading interview: articulating a personal response to texts

Expressing a personal response to a text is regarded as important in the National Curriculum in England. An assessment goal (an 'attainment target') which illustrates this is the following, which is taken from the 'level 3' level descriptions: 'In responding to fiction and non-fiction [pupils] show understanding of the main points and express preferences' (DFE 1995: 28).

Such an attainment target seems reasonable; the difficulty is in deciding when, and under what conditions, a person has met it. As soon as one begins to consider the nature of students' actual responses to what they have read, it becomes clear that while data on personal response can be rich and informative, they may not overlap very readily with summative attainment statements and may be better suited to meeting the teacher's 'local' assessment needs than the 'global' assessment needs of the National Curriculum.

Consider this extract, from an interview one of us taped with a 14-year-old student who will be referred to as 'Emma' (Bailey 1993). Emma is not a student who achieved at a high level in academic terms, but she is an exceptional reader in many respects:

Teacher: Can you tell me how many books you've read in the last month, approximately?

Emma: About . . . probably twenty or more.

Teacher: Probably twenty or more. Now is that a typical amount for you to read in a month?

Emma: Yes.

Teacher: Now could you just, obviously you're not going to be able to remember all of those, just off the top of your head without writing them down, but could you tell me some of the titles that you remember from the last month?

Emma: Yes. Well, I've got several books of my own, new books. There was two, um, Sherlock Holmes books: *The Adventures of Sherlock Holmes* and, er, *The Sign of Four*, by Conan, er. Um, and then there was a book by Francine Pascale, *The Sweet Valley Saga*.

Um, another book by Francine Pascale, *Regina's Legacy*. Then I've got a big thick – that – it's called *The Dark is Rising*, by Susan Cooper, and that's good. And then several other sort of Sweet Dreams books that I read. They're very easy reading. And also from the library I got a *JFK* folder out, 'cause I've just seen the film and so I got the file out of the library and just had a look, basically, at the layout of what happened, first off, 'cause I'm not interested in that kind of thing.

Teacher: Right. Now all of those books that you read you finished, you read from beginning to end, did you?

Emma: Yes.

Teacher: Right. Do you ever give up a book for any reason?

Emma: No.

Teacher: No. Why's that?

Emma: 'Cause even if it's boring it's got, I mean, there must be a reason why they've carried on writing it.

What 'level of personal response' does Emma demonstrate? It's really difficult, and perhaps almost meaningless, to connect Emma's remarks with National Curriculum levels. What do we learn from this brief extract from a thirty-minute interview? We might note the range of her reading, and the fact that she is an avid reader; we could note her categorizing of some texts as 'easy reading', and applaud her understanding of why it can be rewarding to persevere with a book, and her awareness of the author's standpoint.

While this brief interview extract is difficult to connect with national assessment criteria, it has, nevertheless, touched on most of the points listed in our model of responsive assessment:

- the assessment is 'local', and potentially useful for both teacher and student;
- the subjectivity of both teacher and student is valued – indeed one might suggest that it is the nature of the relationship between student and teacher, and the trust which is evident between them, which permits such frankness in the interview to be present;
- the content of what is regarded as evidence of reading achievement is negotiated – Emma chooses the books she wants to discuss;
- the reading activity under discussion is authentic – it is Emma's personal reading.

The two remaining aspects of responsive assessment are:

- evidence of the reader's response is sought and given status;
- the reader's role as a maker of meaning is given status.

These are illustrated in a later extract from the interview:

Teacher: Mm. Does, um, this will be a bit of an unusual question, but when you're not reading, you know, when you're just going about your ordinary life, does anything ever remind you of books that you've read? Do you ever think about books that you've read after you've read them, you know, some time after you've read them?

Emma: Yes. I mean, like this newspaper business [current topic of English lessons]. In the *Sweet Valley High* books there's a school newspaper and it's an American thing, a school newspaper, and that reminded me quite a lot of this, you know. That's why I was quite keen to get into it.

Teacher: Yes. Right. Um, would you, again this is going to be a bit of a weird question, would you say that ever, that reading books helps you to think about your life in any way?

Emma: Yes and no, because sometimes it, in a book, if, like the *Sweet Valley High* books, there's one person in the Sweet Valley High that I'd like to be like. But the thing is, if I was like her then my school work would go down and I wouldn't really be very good at home. You know, I'd be always making excuses, but like, it does help me some ways 'cause like it's like if she does something in one situation it makes me think about what I'd do in that situation. But like, if she, if she tries to get out of something that you, I know that I'd be in trouble for, you know like in one of the books she's making phone calls to people. Um, you know, I'd never do that, but in some ways it makes you think about what would happen if you did make a phone call to somebody. You know, so.

Teacher: So does that mean that you don't have to do it because you can just imagine it?

Emma: You don't have to; the thing is it like puts ideas into your head.

Teacher: Mm.

Emma: Some of the books, um, they're very unrealistic. You know, it's things that wouldn't happen.

Again, it's really difficult to connect Emma's remarks with National Curriculum levels, but there is certainly evidence of personal response, and a clear sense that Emma is able to distance herself from the text. She is aware of realism; she is aware of intertextuality and connects up the fictional newspaper with newspapers in real life and the newspaper in her English lesson project.

In this first case study, then, we have established that an interview can offer plenty of evidence to form the basis of a responsive assessment. In the next case study, we move closer to the classroom, and make some connections between conducting a reading interview and that regular activity in countless classrooms, the book report.

Case study 2: Reading assessment based on interviews developed from children's self-maintained reading records

Earlier in this chapter we boiled our principles for assessment down to four brief questions. In the opening sections of this chapter, we tried to answer question 1). In this case study, we take the final three questions and apply them to a real classroom context.

What are we assessing?

This case study focuses on Year 9 (13- and 14-year-old) secondary school students' wider reading within English lessons. In the case study school, students spend a proportion of their timetabled English lessons in the school library, choosing and reading books and writing and talking about what they have read. The aim of the library lessons, the genesis of which within this particular department pre-dates the introduction of the English National Curriculum, is to develop reading very much as subsequently specified in the current national curriculum programmes of study; these state that for the reading curriculum within English, 'the main emphasis should be on the encouragement of wider reading in order to develop independent, responsive and enthusiastic readers' (DFE 1995: 19).

Library lessons extend the range of wider reading through actively encouraging students to read a range of genres (mostly fictional and/or literary) and to read texts with a thematic or genre link to the current English topic. Each student completes a self-maintained reading record that focuses on his/her own response to the texts that have been read. The reading record provides a focus for informal conversations about reading within the class as well as a basis for occasional semi-formal reading interviews.

The model of reading development implicit here is one which matches well the requirements of a responsive assessment model, in that it privileges independence and personal response. The students are involved in evaluating the range of their reading and their response to it, and setting targets for further reading. The reading assessment focuses on the student's own response to the text and on his/her understanding of genre, character, language and structure. The main emphasis of this assessment is local to the teaching and learning context, assessing of the students' progress and achievements in reading, with respect to the curriculum aims of wider reading in a range of genres and developing response to reading. However, the reading records and interviews, along with other reading activities within English, might also provide evidence for assessing students' English national curriculum levels in reading. (These are reported along with levels in speaking and listening and writing at the end of Year 9 – the end of Key Stage 3 – one of the four national assessment points in a child's school career.)

How is it done?

In Year 9, fifty-minute library lessons occur fortnightly, representing an eighth of English-lesson time. For these lessons the whole class goes to the library with the English teacher and the school librarian. Students return, renew and take out new books in these lessons. They might spend ten minutes choosing a new book, but most of the lesson is spent reading quietly, adding to reading records and talking quietly to peers and the teacher about their reading. Occasionally the librarian or teacher might lead a class discussion on reading. For each book read, whether a book chosen in a library lesson, a book read for another school subject or a book read at home, students complete a short written record. As well as noting the author and title they are asked to identify which genre(s) the book falls into and are given the following prompts for writing a comment: *Write about a character or part of a story you especially liked or disliked. Do not get carried away with retelling the story. It is important to explain WHY you did or did not enjoy this book.*

The reading records are read regularly by teachers in library lessons and students are expected to 'talk to the teacher' when they have read every fifth book, as a minimum. In these interactions teachers will be praising and encouraging students on their reading, making informal formative assessments, such as 'try to explain more why you liked the book', 'what was it about that character that you like?' and 'you need to choose a book from a different genre now'. Students also regularly engage in (or are engaged in) conversation about their reading with the class teacher and with the school librarian, both of whom will make reading recommendations based on their knowledge of particular students. Thus the reading record, within the structure of the library lesson, provides a forum for informal talk about reading which allows teachers to make frequent informal assessments of students' reading habits and response. The conversations between students and teachers also allow the teacher to judge the reliability of a reading record by matching it against the students' spoken comments.

Tape-recorded reading interviews were developed as an extension of this continuity between the written reading records and informal conversations as negotiated assessments within an authentic reading context. The interviews also might elicit further evidence of response, perhaps at a higher (more reflective) level and provide an alternative window on assessment (unconstrained by writing skills). Usually reading interviews had been short and particularly focused on lower ability readers who did not communicate their response successfully in writing. In an attempt to develop wider use of reading interviews a visiting teacher was able to carry out more detailed interviews with a range of students and to compare these with their reading records.

A list of prompt questions was developed for use in reading interviews. The questions were designed to be used as flexible starting points for discussion, alongside the student's own self-assessed reading record. It was considered essential for local assessment needs that the interview structure should not be over formal, as it had to be responsive to each student as an active maker of meaning. A rigidly-controlled structure, although more reliable for making comparisons between students, was not considered appropriate for making formative assessments of students in this context. It is important, however, to be aware of the socially constructed nature of the interview discourse (as indeed of any language-based assessment, including the written reading record) and of the subjectivities of the students and teachers. This is one reason why the interviews were tape-recorded, as this allows analysis of this discourse to be more explicit.

Tape-recorded reading interviews permit students to reflect on their own reading in a way different from how they think when they are producing a written reading record, as we shall argue in relation to extracts from five interviews which follow. The differences may be at the basic level of accuracy of response. 'Andrew', for example, gave an Elton John biography as an example of a book which 'bored' him and which he 'didn't like' in the interview, but he had previously written on his reading record that it was 'very interesting to read'. Three other students said in interviews that they had actually read more than twice the number of books they had indicated on their written records; by contrast, some students revealed during interviews that they had not in fact finished reading books which they had claimed in their reading records to have completed.

Students often write perceptive comments on their reading records. For example:

I found this book [*The Nature of the Beast*] very interesting. I have already read a series of books [stories] by Janni Howker and have found that they have a lot in common particularly dialogue (Andrew).

The book [*A Fatal Inversion*] was written well it kept me interested all the way through and it was very suspenseful (Chris).

I liked the play [*The Secret Diary of Adrian Mole: the Play*] a lot more than the book as it was realistic and a lot more funny (Donna).

This book [*A Breath of Fresh Air*] did not have very interesting characters, but the storyline was good and it was quite sad (Ellie).

Figure 6.1 Wider reading interview: list of possible prompts

1 How many books have you read since the beginning of the school year/the last interview?
2 Can you tell me the titles of some of the books you've read?
3 What genres have you read?
4 Do you have a favourite genre? Why?
5 How do you choose a book to read? Is this different at home to school?
6 What book are you reading at the moment/have you read most recently?
7 How far have you read? – What briefly has happened so far?
8 What do you think is going to happen now/ at the end of the story?
9 Do you get any clues about this in the story? / What makes you think it will end this way? (Slightly more open-ended version)
10 How is it different from what you would like to happen?
11 Ask pupil to read section of book aloud (at teacher's discretion). Can you tell me about the characters in that section? So what would you like to happen to [a character] at the end of the story?
12 Which do you think is the most important character in the book?
13 So how would you describe them – appearance/personality?
14 Why are they important?/What do they do in the story to make them important?
15 Does this character change during the story? How?
16 Are they the most interesting character? Who is?
17 From this and other things you've read, what do you think makes a character interesting/important?
18 Can you think of a place in the story where ___ is particularly interesting/important? OR which is a particularly exciting/sad, etc. part?

However, all these students responded at a more reflective level in the interviews than they did in their written records. This is particularly the case with those students who tend to write very brief comments which are lacking in detail; these students' written comments tend to be characterized by the use of words such as 'good' and 'boring' rather than more specific terms. 'Ben' is described as a low ability student by his teacher and had been identified for special needs support in his first year of secondary schooling. His reading record comments reflect clear preferences, but were very brief and made only general comments about books, for example:

This book [*Diplomatic Deceit*] was quite boring. There wasn't such a good storyline and not enough action.

114

This book [*The Secret Diary of Adrian Mole: the Play*] is not as good as the original and some parts of the book are good but the boring parts outweigh the good.

In his interview, however, Ben reveals that he has read a wider range of genres than indicated on his reading record and he is able to make more sophisticated comments showing an understanding of character and the ability to cite evidence from the text to support his views. At the time of the interview he was reading Tolkien's *The Lord of the Rings*, on his older sister's recommendation. When asked to make predictions, he was able to show that although he doesn't seem to understand the word 'clues' in this context he can in fact identify evidence from the story which has led him to expect a particular plot structure:

Teacher: What do you think is going to happen, from what you've read so far?

Ben: I think the ring'll get lost or he'll throw it away or something, so that the other person can't get it.

Teacher: Are there any clues in the story that might suggest that that's going to happen?

Ben: Not so far.

Teacher: So what makes you think that might happen?

Ben: Just the way he goes about hiding from him, he wants to cover up the ring so . . .

Teacher: So the clues come from what the character's doing.

Ben: Yeah.

Teacher: Right, talking about the character, who is the most important character in the story?

Ben: Bilbo Baggins.

Teacher: Right, what is it that makes him important?

Ben: Well, he's the one with the ring. He's like the main character. Everything revolves around him.

Teacher: Right, can you think of examples of that?

Ben: Well, I read another book with him in and, I don't know what it was called and he had a birthday party and everyone really did what he wanted to do. Like they all came in and when he said something they did it. Nobody else did anything different.

Teacher: So how would you describe Bilbo Baggins?

Ben: And sometimes he can be a bit bossy.

Elsewhere in Ben's reading interview he says that the characters are the most interesting part of the story; this is also the aspect he most wants to talk about. He shows that he has a clear sense of character and can distinguish the roles of two important characters. In comparing the book to others he shows that he does have some understanding of ideas and structure.

Ben: . . . the author's used totally different ideas to any other books I've read. Like he imagines it all himself.

Teacher: Can you say more about that?

Ben: The idea that he's got in the book about goblins and adventures, and the ring.

Teacher: So how do other books compare? What do other books focus on? Like this person's obviously focused on imaginary things.

Ben: Well, one of the books was like focused on one particular aspect of a book and keeps going on and on about it. Well, this one lets you forget about it and then reminds you again.

Teacher: How would you recommend it to someone who hasn't read the story or hasn't heard of it. How would you describe it to somebody else?

Ben: Quite exciting. A lot of imaginative characters. The storyline's quite good.

Another student, 'Francesca', shows a clear progression of preference in her written responses to the three books she has written about on her reading record:

This story [*Nancy Drew – The Ghost of Blackwood Hall*] was very boring but still I read it. I would not read it again.

This book [*There's a Bat in Bunk Five*] is wicked and I would read it again.

This book [*Deanie*] is fantastic. I would definitely read it again and again.

Even though the reading record invites Francesca to comment on character she has not done so, instead restricting herself to her own formulaic style of comment. When encouraged to discuss character in the reading interview, however, she can demonstrate an understanding of the function of the main character within a mystery story:

Teacher: In the mystery book was there a main character?

Francesca: Yeah, that girl.

Teacher: Why do you think she was the main character? What was it about her that made her important?

Francesca: I don't know, it was because she's done everything and every time you read a bit she was in it, like she was the one who solves the problems.

Teacher: Can you think of a particular part of the story that shows she was important? Or showed that she was interesting to you? Or made you think 'yeah, that reminds me of me'?

Francesca: She went with a friend and she was walking a dog through this forest and she like seen a man and she heard a scream and she wanted to follow it so she walked through the wood and she couldn't and then she found these footsteps and she followed all them footsteps. And I found that really interesting.

Teacher: Do you think she was the most interesting character in the story?

Francesca: No, I think that the auntie was because she was killed and everything and it tells you most stuff about her, and the case, when she gets the case from the office, she reads things about her.

Teacher: What do you think makes a character interesting?

Francesca: Just what they do and the story. If they've got good parts. They say more things than other characters.

Teacher: Now then, can you think about a situation, for example the situation when that girl was following the footsteps, why do you think she actually did that? Do you think she had a reason for doing that?

Francesca: Yeah, like she was the detective. Like she was like undercover and she's not meant to be and all she was doing was walking the dog and the next minute she heard a scream so she thought she'd follow the scream and then she came up solving something.

The use made of the assessment data

Tape-recorded reading interviews clearly provide a rich source of information about students' reading progress from a different perspective from that of the self-maintained reading record. The students are able to express their response in a more tentative and exploratory way in speech, as opposed to the less correctable form of a written comment, particularly if they are limited in their writing skills. The teacher conducting the interview can encourage students to elaborate a response, or ask a question in different ways in order to allow a student to demonstrate his or her understanding.

Of course, an interview is a socially constructed event and one in which the teacher has more status than the student. It is possible that the teacher might be guiding students to produce certain responses; similarly students may say what they think the teacher wants to hear. Either of these processes, occurring either consciously or unconsciously, might make it seem that students understand something they do not or have thought something

117

they have not. The teacher needs to be aware of this tension, but it is not a reason for not using interviews as one methodology of reading assessment, and a particularly illuminating one. Not asking prompt questions increases the risk of limiting the assessment of students' abilities to what they demonstrate spontaneously or to what they perceive as what the teacher wants to hear or read. It is certainly the case that the written reading record has its own writing conventions, just as the students have their own assumptions about what it should contain. However much teachers urge students to write more exploratory and personal comments, with reasons for their views, our experience has been that a large proportion of students tend to use language which is more appropriate to a published book review, with recommendations and star ratings. It is interesting to consider why students do this and what audience is implied by such comments. As teachers assessing our students in classroom contexts we need to be aware of the constructedness of evidence and the discourse of reading records, interviews and other forms of communication which occur in the classroom.

We feel there are many good reasons for using reading interviews: they tell us something worthwhile about students' progress and can suggest implications for subsequent teaching. In this school the interviews have enabled teachers to see that some students have more sophisticated understanding of books than had been thought. The teachers were able to guide the students' future reading choices and to have higher expectations for future discussion about texts. The students come to see themselves as better readers and become more willing to talk about their reading, partly because they feel that someone has taken an interest in them as readers.

This case study also highlights the importance of finding an alternative to written assessment tasks, which disadvantage many students. As well as serving this local, formative assessment purpose, the interviews also provided evidence which helped the teachers to assign national curriculum reading assessment levels and, in some cases, higher ones than they would have felt justified in giving without the interview data. In this school, reading interviews have contributed valuably to the range of more authentic approaches to assessment and teachers have also found it possible to use interview data in relation to national assessment procedures.

Any classroom teacher reading the two case studies which we have shared thus far in this chapter is likely to have one major reservation – and this concerns the time needed to interview students. We accept that this is a severe limitation. In the case-study school, interviews generally take place no more frequently than once per student per year, and tape-recording has been used only on an experimental basis. One partial solution to this problem of teacher time is to put more emphasis on the students' self-assessment and peer-assessment, and it is this which is the focus of our third case study.

Case study 3: Using the tape-recorder for self- and peer-assessment in the primary classroom

In this school, an inner-city junior school, children have been using tape-recorders as part of reading assessment, particularly self-assessment. The theoretical issues dealt with earlier in this chapter have underpinned the work, but many of the challenges faced by the school and the students have been practical ones.

Attention has focused on the following key issues: the ownership of reading assessment data, the problems of handling the technology, the importance of modelling responses to reading, and the issue of long-term evaluation. In addressing these issues, the school gave all students in the pilot classes (most of whom were 10 years old at the beginning of the school year) their own tape, for which they had responsibility, and which would remain their property when they left the school, if they so wished.

Problems of handling the technology of the tape-recorder are not easy for 10-year-olds, and these together with problems of managing the house-keeping of tape-recorded data, were addressed through weekly whole-class discussion sessions. The teachers worked to develop the students' skills in listening to each other, since such skills are an essential prerequisite for peer assessment. These skills were developed initially through whole-class discussion of brief presentations made to their classmates by each student on a character from their favourite TV soap opera. This whole-class activity was undertaken in order to provide a model of discussion activities which could be later generalized to comments on stories and characters from books which the students had read and which might form part of a tape-recorded evaluation of a book made in an individual or small-group context.

The children discussed how the tapes might be used and it became plain that, in seeking to retain evidence of their long-term development as a reader, many of the students were keen to simply record themselves reading aloud. It seemed likely, therefore, that the recordings would provide direct evidence of individuals' reading fluency as well as information on their response to reading.

Having the students take part in this activity was an important component of the teacher's plan for her class over the whole year, and was part of a wider emphasis on self-assessment within the school and across the curriculum. At the end of the year, the children evaluated the assessment procedures with which they had been involved and stated consistently that they preferred assessment procedures in which they were actively involved in making judgements about their own progress. The class teacher was certain that working on self-assessment had increased motivation and improved student behaviour; one interesting spin-off was that some students felt confident enough to request that the teacher moved them to a 'slower' or 'faster' group for some activities.

Many children reported that when they initially started to be involved in the tape-recording, they felt anxious about the responsibility for making judgements about their peers and were concerned to support rather than criticize their fellow students. They came to recognize that it took skill to be able to ask a good question of a classmate. Finally – and the teacher was delighted to report this – by the end of the school year, the children were becoming confident enough to challenge the teacher's own assessment of their reading ability. In a final session, the class teacher asked the students what their final thoughts were which they would like to pass on to the university. The students came up with eight points:

- You can be an independent improver.
- You are more confident as a speaker.
- You will be interesting to listen to in later years.
- You become less self-conscious.
- You try harder because you are being recorded.
- You learn some information technology as well as reading.
- You get more involved with a group.
- You enjoy doing it.

The approach to the responsive assessment of reading which has been sketched in this third case study places a good deal of faith in data obtained from students using a tape recorder independently of the teacher. There are, of course, many reasons for being cautious about such an approach:

1   Tape-recordings in school produce 'situated discourse':
- students may say what they think the teacher wishes to hear;
- students may simply repeat curriculum goal outlines which they have been taught;
- not every student interviews well (for reasons ranging from shyness to subversion);
- there may be a poor match between actual reading behaviours and taped discourse;
- teachers (or others) may guide the discourse inappropriately.

2   Making recordings in school is not a simple matter:
- training, discussion and practice are necessary;
- housekeeping rules are necessary;
- students may have difficulties with the technology of the tape-recorder;
- valuable data may be unintentionally erased or lost;
- older students may erase tape sections they feel uncomfortable with.

3   Questions of ownership and the use made of data are not simple:

- who really does own the tapes?
- what role does negotiation play?
- how does the student identify 'next steps'?
- how should the teacher support the students' 'next steps'?

Even if all the above problems are addressed, there remains the crucial issue of how the evidence gathered using classroom-based responsive assessment approaches connects up with the imperatives of 'high stakes' assessment. One possibility is to accept the argument that there *is* a fundamental incompatibility between developmental assessment and high stakes assessment. However, while the high stakes assessment initiatives associated with the National Curriculum in England have been a cause for great concern, the National Curriculum itself has been generally accepted as offering a fairly reasonable basis for setting developmental assessment targets. What one would want to suggest, therefore, is that the approaches reported in this chapter are not doomed simply because they are occurring within a larger coercive framework.

Conclusions

Our conclusions section is very brief. The early part of this chapter advanced the concept of responsive assessment; the case studies offered some illustrations of it in action. Is it sensible to develop such approaches at a time when some governments are advocating a return to more traditional tests? Certainly – since political will cannot ultimately continue to use what is unworkable. Meanwhile, responsive assessment of reading can proceed on a small-scale basis very successfully: it can contribute to the attempt to shift the project of assessment from a 'global' to a 'local' level, and if there are difficulties in generalizing from data gathered at the 'local' level, one must accept that such difficulties are unavoidable.

The issue is not so much that it may be invalid to make generalized statements based on responsive assessment data, but rather that we need to accept that in attempting to make such statements we are rethinking the concept of generalizability. This is a tall order, however, since to rethink the concept of generalizability is to embark on a rethinking of the whole concept of validity in reading assessment. However, we would argue that such a reconceptualization is long overdue.

References

Bailey, M. (1993) *Children's Response to Fiction*, M.Ed. dissertation, University of Nottingham.

Clarke, K. (1990) Personal communication. Meeting at the Department of Education and Science with representatives of UKRA, NATE, the Book Trust and the Association of Advisers and Inspectors for English.

Department of Education and Science (DES)(1990) *English in the National Curriculum* (No.2), London: HMSO.

Department for Education (DFE) (1995) *English in the National Curriculum*, London: HMSO.

Eagleton, T. (1983) *Literary Theory*, Oxford: Basil Blackwell.

Harrison, C., Bailey, M. and Dewar, A. (1998) 'Responsive Reading Assessment: is postmodern assessment of reading possible?' in C. Harrison and T. Salinger *Assessing Reading 1: Theory and Practice*, London: Routledge.

Johnston, Peter (1993) 'Assessment as social practice. National Reading Conference annual review of research', in D.J. Leu and C.K. Kinzer (eds) *Examining Central Issues in Literacy Research, Theory and Practice,* Forty-second Yearbook of the National Reading Conference, Chicago: National Reading Conference.

LATE (1995) *The Real Cost of SATs*, London: London Association for the Teaching of English.

McGregor, R. and Meirs, M. (1991) *Telling the Whole Story,* Hawthorne, Victoria: Australian Council for Educational Research.

Ruddock, G., Brooks, G., Harris, D., Salt, S., Putman, K. and Schagen, I (1995) *Evaluation of National Curriculum Assessment in English and Technology at Key Stage 3: 1993,* Slough, Berkshire: National Foundation for Educational Research.

Stake, R.E. (1979) 'Program evaluation, particularly responsive evaluation', in W. Dockrell and D. Hamilton (eds) *Rethinking Educational Research,* London: Hodder & Stoughton.

7

THE LITERACY PROFILE OF
MAXWELL POGONOWSKI

Patricia G. Smith

This chapter attempts to explore the complex relationship between learning, teaching, assessing and reporting by considering the work of one 11-year-old boy, Maxwell Pogonowski. Any students' conceptions about the nature, purposes and functions of reading, writing, speaking and listening are the result of interaction between their prior knowledge and language events experienced in the classroom, as well as in the world. Assessment and reporting, it is argued here, should result from similar interactions.

Multiple contexts for assessment are available in every classroom. They provide for many types of observations and rely on many types of validity. The teacher is in control of decisions regarding what competencies are valued in the school context, and so selects appropriate assessment procedures. Attitudes, interests and other affective characteristics so necessary for learning to be successful are able to be assessed if teacher judgement is part of the process. By following the methods of action researchers, ethnographers, anthropologists and others who study human behaviour in natural settings and seek rich data, teachers can use assessment which is matched to the learning, as a number of chapters in this volume demonstrate. It is authentic.

It is customary to describe the three-part process used by researchers to observe behaviour as triangulation. This approach may be applied to assessment and reporting in schools. The first part involves identifying the significant features, such as teaching and learning contexts and goals; the second is an intensive observation of practice; the third is a theoretical study of principles such as predicted performances and learning development. Cross-disciplinary triangulation allows similar skills demonstrated in different subject areas to be assessed. Repeated observation uses the same assessment over many occasions to observe the same behaviour. These triangulation methods may be used together to increase the possibility of obtaining a more consistent and more valid assessment that contains sufficient information to suit everybody's needs and purposes.

Triangulation is based on a premise that no one type of measure can adequately describe any phenomenon being described. A series of related observations using a different referent for the performance is likely to provide credible – or valid – information. The teacher can use a literacy profile scale which encourages the use of multiple methods of observation and which provides criterion-referenced descriptions to organize these observations. In simple terms, a profile is a scale depicting progress in learning. An essential feature of a student's profile is that it shows growth. Through its ordered sequence of events, it makes explicit what progress in learning means. It provides a framework against which evidence of progress of an individual can be charted and the achievements of a school – or even an education system – can be monitored. A profile enables assessment to be a natural part of teaching and learning because the data are collected when the teaching and learning are taking place (Griffin, 1989).

Literacy profiling began in Victoria, Australia when the Ministry of Education instigated a search for a system of monitoring achievement in schools. After almost five years of research and development, the first Victorian *Literacy Profile Handbook* appeared and it has been followed by the similar development of the *American Literacy Profile Scales* (Griffin, Smith and Bunill, 1995). The Australian National Profiles grew out of these first profiles. After several years of the successful monitoring of school achievements it became clear that profiling also has a positive effect on teaching and learning.

Other researchers have explored the complex relationship between learning, teaching, assessment and reporting. Clay (1979, 1991), Goodman (1973, 1985, 1993), Harste, Woodward and Burke (1984) and Harste, Short and Burke (1988) are among those who have stressed the importance of teachers' making detailed observations of children's literacy behaviours which demonstrate this close relationship. There is a strong basis for the belief that these observations are even more helpful if they include the students' own views. Children's learning takes place as they appropriate for themselves those aspects of literate behaviour that are learnt socially. Harste *et al.* (1984) and Bruner (1986) emphasize the importance of the relationship between individuals and their social context; they engage in a collaborative problem-solving process, making sense of the situation and constructing new understandings.

Focus on Max: gathering information at the beginning of the school year

The starting point for gathering information is the collection of classroom observations of student behaviours. The observations may be made by the teachers and the students themselves. This chapter focuses on one particular student, Max, to demonstrate how a profile is developed. Max was aged 11 and in grade 6 when the information was gathered.

Reading and writing inventories begin to involve the student in the information-gathering process. Here are Max's answers in the reading inventory at the beginning of the year:

Q: Do you like reading?
A: Yes, I like reading because it's fun and because of the fact that if you don't like the book you're reading you can put it down and get a different one.
Q: What do you read?
A: I like reading big books like Tolkien and adventure, mystery books like Enid Blyton because things like that get me hooked on.
Q: When you are reading and you come to something you can't read what do you do?
A: I haven't come upon any unreadable word lately so I can't really say.
Q: Who are good readers you know?
A: Only Dad and I really.
Q: What makes them good readers?
A: The reason I am a good reader is that when I was young and Mum read to me I followed the words.
Q: If you know someone having trouble reading how would you help them?
A: I would sort of read one page and let them read the next.
Q: How would you become a better reader.
A: To become a better reader I only have to read more.

From his reading inventory it can be seen that Max thinks, like many others, including teachers, that he will get better at reading if he reads more books which increase in difficulty. Although attitudes and response to literature are important aspects of a reader's profile Max does not indicate any need to discuss these indicators as part of improving his reading.

Max has many interests, being a keen sportsman and a talented musician who sings in the choir and plays the piano, guitar and the saxophone. He has many experiences to bring to his reading. Max wrote in his writing inventory that he particularly enjoys writer's workshop times and wants to be a writer like his father. His mother, who is a volunteer literature-group helper, is a keen reader and they often talk about books together. Evidence has accumulated about social, cultural and cognitive beliefs about what reading meant to Max, and similarly to the other students.

Max's literacy profile at the beginning of the year

The teacher begins to form a picture of Max's reading strategies and habits from the reading inventory, observations, end-of-year descriptive reports by his previous teacher and from his parents. This information would be very unwieldy but for the indicators on the scale, which provide a manageable way of rating progress. The indicators are evidently present in the student's work and they provide a common vocabulary for describing progress. The indicators on this scale were developed by teachers as they observed their students. Figure 7.1 shows an interpretation of Max's reading development at the beginning of the school year. The italicized statements indicate those which teachers shaded in for Max.

At the beginning of the year Max provided an example of a very keen 11-year-old reader. Max had established all reading behaviours indicated in

Figure 7.1   Reading bands C, D, E and F. The American literacy profile scales

---

Band   Reading

C   Reading strategies
Reads a paragraph or a sentence to establish meaning. Uses context as a basis for predicting meaning of unfamiliar words. Reads aloud showing understanding of purpose of punctuation marks. Uses picture clues to make appropriate responses for unknown words. Uses pictures to help read a text. Finds where another reader is up to in a reading passage.

Responses
Writing and artwork reflect understanding of text. Retells, discusses and expresses opinions on literature and reads further. Recalls events and characters spontaneously from text.

Interest and attitudes
Seeks recommendations for books to read. Chooses more than one type of book. Chooses to read when given free choice. Concentrates on reading for lengthy periods.

D   Reading Strategies
Reads material with a wide variety of styles and topics. *Selects books to fulfil own purposes.* States main idea in a passage. *Substitutes words with similar meanings when reading aloud. Self-corrects, using knowledge of language structure and sound-symbol relationships.* Predicts, using knowledge of language structure and/or sound symbol relationships to make sense of a word or phrase.

Responses
Discusses different types of reading materials. *Discusses materials read at home. Tells a variety of audiences about a book. Uses vocabulary and sentence structure from reading materials in written work as well as in conversation.* Themes from reading appear in art work. *Follows written instructions.*

continued . . .

Interest and attitudes

Recommends books to others. Reads often. Reads silently for extended periods.

E   Reading Strategies

Reads to others with few inappropriate pauses. Interprets new words by reference to suffixes, prefixes and meaning of word parts. Uses directories such as a table of contents or an index, or telephone and street directories, to locate information. Uses library classification systems to find specific reading materials.

Responses

Improvises in role play, drawing on a range of text. Writing shows meaning inferred from the text. *Explains a piece of literature.* Expresses and supports an opinion on whether an author's point of view is valid. Discusses implied motives of characters in the text. Makes comments and expresses feelings about characters. *Rewrites information from text in own words.* Uses text as a model for own writing. *Uses a range of books and print materials as information sources for written work. Reads aloud with expression.*

F   Reading Strategies

Describes links between personal experience and arguments and ideas about text. *Selects relevant passages or phrases to answer questions without necessarily reading the whole text. Formulates research topics and questions and finds relevant information from reading materials.* Maps out plots and character development in novels and other literary texts. *Varies reading strategies according to purposes for reading and nature of text.* Makes connections between texts, recognizing similarities of themes and values.

Responses

Discusses author's intent for the reader. Discusses styles used by different authors. Describes settings in literature. Forms generalizations about a range of genres, including myth, short stories. Offers reasons for the feelings provoked by a text. Writing and discussions acknowledge a range of interpretations of text. Offers critical opinion or analysis of reading passages in discussion. Justifies own appraisal of a text. Synthesizes and expands on information from a range of texts in written work.

band C, was developing those in bands D and E and was beginning to use some of the strategies listed in band F. These indicators synthesize much of the information that is able to be gained intuitively from the above description. Max was shown to be a reader who can talk about what he has read. He absorbs language and ideas. He knows how to tackle a difficult text and read silently for extended periods.

Compiling the data

Individual profiles showed that Max and the other students in the grade were all readers who had already learnt how to use the semantic, syntactic and graphophonic cueing systems described in a sociopsycholinguistic approach to reading (Goodman 1970). It was in the areas of response and attitude that there was a lack of progress in the grade's reading development. The process of compiling data had been of formative use in that it helped the teacher see the need to look closely at her program. Here was a method of assessment which had positive washback effects.

Planning new arrangements for learning

Wells (1986) has argued that it is not possible to specify in advance the path which learning will follow. The student's role as partner in the educational process should, therefore, be acknowledged. Instead of conceptualizing teaching as a process which requires the teacher to carefully select and sequence input for a student there should be an emphasis on providing supportive contexts. Teaching should be viewed as 'essentially a matter of facilitating learners, and where that learning depends on communication between the teacher and learner, the principles apply as in any successful conversation. The aim must be the collaborative construction of meaning, with negotiation to ensure that meanings are mutually understood' (Wells 1986:101).

In supportive contexts, students learn how to solve problems and to use reading, writing, talking, listening and viewing as tools for learning. Although these language modes are seen as objects worthy of study in their own right, the contexts also stress language in use and provide for *learning language, learning about language* and *learning through language* as natural components. The use of supportive contexts acknowledges the social nature of language and language learning. It follows that the students' own reflections on their learning are also an important part of the assessment and reporting process.

While reading provides the main focus for the development of Max's profile because it is the language mode which was of particular concern to his teacher, it will be seen that writing and especially listening and speaking have an integral part to play in the discussion.

Observing Max in context: a book talk

Literature groups are quite common contexts in literature-based reading programmes. They are structured in many ways and allow for reader-response activities. Students are organized to read common texts. At other times these small group sessions are used for similar activities using the books individually chosen by the students. They may prepare book talks to give to the rest of their small group. They are expected to keep their reading logs up-to-date in these sessions or during homework time. Students also use homework time to complete the reading of a chapter.

The following text is an excerpt from a book talk session about self-chosen texts in small groups.

Max: I read John Marsden, *Out of Time*, and it's about this boy called James who finds this crooked time machine that … creating in the lab and at the moment he's just found out how to use it and he went all dizzy at one point because there's a magnetic force field being used.

Amber: Why did he make a magnetic force field?

Max: Because he wanted a pocket time machine.

Matthew: Does the pocket time machine work?

Max: I don't know. The pocket time machine was as big as a calculator.

   (Max does not want to answer a question because it was too broad and required too much effort for a 'no real need to know' question. The accepted pattern of question and answer has been broken, but Max thinks of an answer that will deal with the question. He indicates there is a great deal of technology in a small space.)

Jessica: Who's the main character?

Max: James.

Matthew: How old is he?

Max: About my age.

Ben: Who's the author?

Max: John Marsden.

None of the students had the book open, or even in their hands. The students had developed a formula for book-sharing sessions. They were asking ritualistic questions, which were occasionally repeated. Max had given the name of the author and then Ben asked, 'Who is the author?' Similarly, Max was asked 'Who's the main character?' twice.

Rosenblatt (1978) argues that a reader is always actively engaged in making meaning; that meaning resides neither in the reader, nor in the text, but is constantly renewed in a reader's transaction with the text. The chosen activities were not helping the students take part in making transactions with texts. The literature groups needed to be restructured so that students would be engaged in real talk about books.

Observing Max in a discussion group led by the teacher

Teacher dominance of talk is a well-known phenomenon. In the previous discussion it was shown that the students had developed a format which used formulaic questions as an appropriate way to organize discussion. How did they learn to do this? A number of studies have identified a characteristic initiate-respond-feedback exchange structure as the basic unit of discourse in most lessons, especially those involving large groups of students. In such exchanges the teacher initiates the interaction and provides the feedback. The pupil, for the most part, only plays the role of respondent. The following extract is taken from a discussion session early in the year:

Teacher: But what sort of character is he?
Max: Mean and old.
Amber: He wants you to make all these deals like that if he's. . .
Teacher: Why is he interested in making the deals though?
Kirsten: Because all he probably cares about is the underground.
Daniel: It's his, he wants this and he wants that.
Luke: He's sort of a mean and old person because some old people are . . .
Teacher: Why is he so involved with the underground?
Luke: Because he thinks that that's the only good place, he doesn't think that . . .
Teacher: Why is it so important to him?

The teacher asked the questions, so led the discussion. Max takes his turn at answering a question. This discourse implies that the teacher knew what the 'correct' responses would be; the questions often required the students to display knowledge already possessed by the teacher. They were, once again, not real need-to-know questions.

Teachers may also be heard organizing discussions. They give turns and they control behaviour. This typical classroom behaviour needed to be changed if the students were to have real conversations. They would have to take responsibility for their own behaviour. The teacher would thus have to step back.

Decisions following the observations of learning contexts

The teacher learned that Max was able to describe the elements of a text such as the main character, the plot and the setting, but the format of the book talk as it had been culturally constructed in her classroom was not allowing him to show how he had transacted with the text. There was also no opportunity for meaning to be socially constructed, or reconstructed, in these monologic sessions. Other than telling them that it was a good book to read, Max had not tried any other means of persuasion.

Similarly, in the session with the teacher, Max and the others were still engaged in monologue rather than in a real dialogue (Bahktin, 1988). The big question was whether there are useful strategies that could be learned so that readers in grade five/six would be helped to transact with, reconstruct and interpret literary texts for themselves without the teacher leading the discussion. Resolving the question of what readers must do to transact with texts was the first step. We read literature by attending to our subjective responses, or our likes and dislikes, by connecting patterns and by acknowledging and working through the puzzles and problems evoked by the text. As we read in this way we enjoy the real pleasures of reading aesthetically because we know how to think about our thinking as we read.

Introducing a new supportive context for learning

Aidan Chambers (Chambers 1993) designed a *Tell Me* strategy that would 'scaffold' learners so that they would be able to take on the learning by themselves and this strategy became a useful way of mediating learning during the year. Picture story books are great to work with because they incorporate so much in a few pages. The teacher read to the students and had them brainstorm their responses under the headings, 'I like', 'I dislike', 'Patterns' and 'Puzzles' and connect their responses across the columns. These connections were briefly discussed in the large group before the students chose the connection they wished to discuss in small groups.

It was hypothesized that work in small groups, without the teacher, would allow the students to test their initial responses within these secure confines. Collaborative construction opportunities would allow them to clarify and refine their responses and to obtain the confirmation they needed to develop trust in their intuition and the relevance of their experience. The teacher deliberately moved away from the forefront of the large group, and withdrew altogether from the small group discussions, in order to assign the students full responsibility for the meanings to be made. Students were expected to carry on the usual practices of a conversation, including taking part without putting up their hands for a turn.

It was hoped that evidence would appear of the students deliberately using the ways to talk about literature to which they had been introduced. A pattern of discourse needed to be established which would support this view of dialogic interaction rather than the monologic discourse they had been using.

Evidence of dialogue rather than monologue in group discussions about books

The students soon showed that they could use these new ways to understand literature. Max in this sequence from a small-group discussion at the beginning of Rosemary Sutcliff's *The Shield Ring* is the first to draw attention to the harp. There is a joint understanding developed that the harp will have a role to play and that it will be part of a pattern. During the discussion the students where appropriate support their statements with reasons from the text or from prior knowledge showing that they have internalized from earlier experiences how to develop the discussion. They know how language works in the new classroom culture which is being established.

Max:	Maybe he carries that little harp around with him and it makes everybody dance when they hear it.
Liam:	And when people are attacking him, he plays it and he makes them dance.
Kirsten:	It could be like from the piper.
Max:	He couldn't make the shiny sounds with the harp until he really knows how to use it, until he treats the harp properly. It's like the harp's sort of alive and it's got feelings and if you don't treat it properly it won't play properly.
Kirsten:	If it is going to be like that then it's probably going to be a bit like the piper, because when he played his flute, he made everybody dance and made everybody follow him, so if it is going to be something like Max said with the harp, then it's probably going to be a bit like the Pied Piper.
Amber:	It's like all the mice came. It could be like people like gods and all that come and help him.
Max:	I don't really think it will be about magic because it's about Vikings and Vikings didn't really have magic.
Daniel:	It's going to be real life stuff.
Amber:	I don't think it's about magic because the Romans and the Vikings they fight.
Liam:	All the Vikings they mainly cause fights. It might be just real life stuff.
Kirsten:	Why the music then?
Stephanie:	They might not think you can get peace. They might not know what peace means.
Amber:	I think that Liam is right because the Romans and the Vikings. All they do is just fight and I think the music might bring them peace.
Max:	You think that the people that play the harp, maybe it makes them stop fighting and just to think about it, just to listen to the music they stop fighting. Music is a kind of magic when it does this.

This discussion may have seemed to be going in the wrong direction with its talk of magic harps and Pied Pipers and it would be second nature for a teacher to break in and lead them along a straightforward track, but they travelled to understanding by a more circuitous route, using another text that had a theme of the power of music. The students have learned to be confident that an author uses patterns in a text which they will have read in texts by other authors for the reader to use to support meaning. Max appears to have internalized this strategy as he works towards his statement about the power of music being stronger than the power of the sword, or in this case, the battle-axe.

Developing new strategies: imagery and voices in the mind

Max learned to use many other cognitive strategies to make meaning. One of the most interesting was the use of imagery to describe thinking. References to 'pictures in the mind' were frequent in the small-group discussions. Max and the others were quite clear that their images were developed to work with the text or the author to build the text world. They also seemed to accept that different images were possible, according to their past experiences. Max had worked out that the pictures are the voices in his mind.

Max: The more you understand the book, the more coloured and full the pictures get in your mind. Like when you're reading at the start we didn't understand much, like you'd get black-and-white pictures, fairly small ones, but now that you understand more then you get better pictures in your head. I don't really get just pictures in my head. It's like a proper movie. You've got this screen and you get it all. It's all your thoughts whizzing around, flashing in your head.

Near the end of the year, Max struggles to explain the fast time phase of imaging where the reader is not being faced with any anomalies that would require 'slowed down' thinking.

Max: Yes, when I read in my mind I don't realize that I'm reading it and I don't realize that I'm hearing the story. I just go along as it is and think of the pictures in my head. . . .
Hayley: Like non stop reading.
Richard: Yes, you just keep reading until you get tired or something.
Max: It feels like you're watching the movies 'cause you're reading it to yourself and you're reading it fast and you've got the picture in your head straight away.

Another view of learning: writing in a journal

Talk in small groups provided multiple opportunities for observing students trying out and formulating their ideas. Writing did have some value, too. The students were often asked to work from their original responses in the large-group discussion and write a fuller and/or more organized statement which would be useful in the small-group discussions. The students did find that it was useful to write briefly to organize thought for discussion.

This is Max's journal entry after large-group reading of Gary Crew's and Greg Rogers' picture story book *Lucy's Bay*:

> I think the illustrations in this book were terrific. I can't see how all different sorts of drawing materials can make a picture that looks so real. The illustrator obviously talked to the writer first. In this book Sam goes to a bay that his sister died in that he had been afraid of. He finds her memorial stone and looks at it for a first time. It was very sad. It would have been very hard if you had wanted to do something else and you left your sister for a minute and she drowned in the sea. He had to see the stone to get his memory back and get over the tragedy.

Max reports on his learning development: portfolios and self-evaluation

Students develop portfolios to record work required, points of organization and, especially, reflections about learning. Examples of interest, planning, research, writing and presentation of learning projects are included. 'I put this in my portfolio because it shows. . .'.

Examples follow of three items Max chose to include in his portfolio to demonstrate his learning. He as a reader became an inquirer or ethnographer as he defined himself in relation to his reading.

Item 1. What do you do if you find a sea bird with oil on it?

> When you find the bird approach it slowly and throw a towel over it. Pick it up gently still using the towel. When you have carried it back slowly get a large box big enough for it to move around, put newspaper in the bottom. DO NOT USE GRASS OR STRAWLIKE THINGS. Grass and straw will cause lung disease. Change newspaper regularly. To feed, pry open beak gently.

What I know about fairy penguins.

Scientists call fairy penguins 'Little Blue'.

The fairy penguin's preen gland is something that you squeeze and oil comes out so the penguin puts its beak on it and they get oil and they clean their feathers with it.

If a penguin drinks salt water the salt goes through its nose.

The sea creatures that eat penguins are sharks, killer whales and sea leopards.

When a penguin is between 0 weeks and 8 weeks they have a white ruff.

When a penguin is small the mother and father drop the food into the penguin's mouth.

The fairy penguin also dives in and out of the water to play.
*I chose this report about Fairy Penguins and how to help oil-covered birds because it shows that I can do research and write up what I have learnt. I still need to find out why the young penguins have a white ruff and what the success rate is for helping birds with oil on them.

Item 2.   Final reading inventory

Q: What is reading?
A: Reading is. . . . um, no, I won't start that way. I'll start at the beginning. For me that is.

I started reading at about four years old when Mum was still reading to me. All I knew about it then was looking at the pictures. I was really curious about those wiggly lines on the paper so I asked Mum which wiggly line she was on. After that I kept following Mum's finger while she was reading. That's how I learnt.

In my reading log you will find evidence that I like reading Tolkien's books but it takes me so long to absorb all the wonderful text that it takes a long time to finish. I suggested 'The Hobbit' to Dan and Jacob but they don't enjoy it as much as me. 1. 'Cause maybe it's not the type of writing they like. 2. Because they probably don't read in as much depth as I do. These are also the probable reasons that they whizz through it (no offence guys).

Now I will make a list.

Reading is working out what the writer said in the story.

Reading is information or just a story.

Reading is what you can relate to.

Sometimes the start is boring.

Reading can be comics, fairy tales and other things.

Reading is fun, enjoyable and when you are in bed and you are reading you know what is going to happen because your eyes skim and you want to read more and more.

Reading is being in the story.

Reading is relaxing.

Your brain works out what the words are while you are reading.

Reading is having pictures and puzzles and working out the patterns.

Reading is wanting to talk about it.

Q: What did you learn to do in reading this year?

A: During the year we've read a lot of books and talked about them. We talk about the book to understand what it's about. Now I find that reading gets easier as you put more pieces to the puzzle and that a good deal of books leave a number of pieces out but sometimes you just haven't noticed them. When I read books to myself like I sometimes talk to people about it to help me understand what the book's about. Before I used to talk about what was happening or the things I liked. I also have learned to listen and talk in my head. I can make pictures in it too and they help me think about different questions that come into my head.

When I write stories I always read it through. When I read through it helps me understand what I'm writing better. I seem to understand what I am trying to say.

Now I understand a lot more about reading. Talking about books helps me understand them better.

Q: What happens when you read?

A: When we read a book the picture that I get in my head gives me an idea for what is going on. When we read The Lake at the End of the World the talk together made me understand the puzzles that I had. Some books that I have read I do not understand at the beginning and they're hard but I find when I get to the middle of the book I feel that it is much easier. When I read a book I have pictures in my head. At the end of the Lake at the End of the World I could see the Councillor sitting there but the picture was wrong. When we found out he was dead I thought, 'Yes!'. I like to write it down in my journal and it makes it easier for me to think. I love to read and to talk about the book I have read. I like to read long books.

Q: How would you help somebody become a better reader?

A: Well, I would make them sound out the beginning of the word to help them find one that makes sense if they were having trouble. After they have finished I would [tell] them what did they feel if somebody picked up a book and it was a hard book. It may be good to talk about it to make them understand more. Pictures in your head help you understand a lot more than just writing. You can relate to things in books.

*I wanted to put the end-of-the year Reading Inventory into my portfolio because it shows how much I have learned about reading this year. You will see this when you compare this one with the first one.

At the beginning of the year I said I would help someone by telling them to sound out the words. We can all do that, or just read on. Now I know about pictures and talk in my head. It is not wasting time to do this. I found out that if you talk with others and listen to what they think this makes everyone understand better.

136

Item 3. A copy of talk about Edward the Emu

Max: Well the story gives it away that he wants to be the best because the man said he'd rather look at the lions. So Edward rushes off to be a lion.

Sasha: He goes to the lions then he's going to whatever other animals they say.

Hayley: He wants to get the crowd's attention.

Daniel: It'd get him down, don't you think, if somebody said that?

Max: He wants to show off and be the best.

Kirsten: But how come nobody notices that he's an emu, he's different. People don't say, 'Oh look at that emu in the lion's cage or look at that emu in the seal's. . . .'

Max: He's a populist.

Elizabeth: What does that mean?

Max: He wants to be what ever anyone wants him to be. But that's not a good idea. You can't please everyone. It's better to be yourself.
* We talk about books in groups and have the recorder going. We listen to ourselves if we want to find out how we are going. This part shows I can make some good points as we work out what a book means. We all have different ideas and get them from each other.

Max's own views are important because of the complex relationship that has been demonstrated between the student's knowledge and thinking to teaching. The student's conception about reading, its nature, purposes and functions, are a result of interaction between prior knowledge and feelings about reading and the reading events experienced in the classroom.

The teacher reports on Max's progress

An enormous amount of information had been collected about Max as his knowledge of the reading process expanded. Indicators of development accumulated in an observable fashion as the students' reading abilities progressively emerged and their knowledge of the reading process expanded. The teacher used a highlighter pen to add to the list of attributes grouped in bands in the reading profile scales (Griffin, Smith and Burrill 1995). (Teachers usually use a different colour to indicate new areas of growth.) Figure 7.2 illustrates Max's progress on a 'reading profile rocket'.

Max provided rich criteria for the assessment and reporting of his learning. The gist statements for each band of indicators provide a pen picture of his growth and the rocket shows this diagrammatically.

Figure 7.2 Reading profile rocket – Max

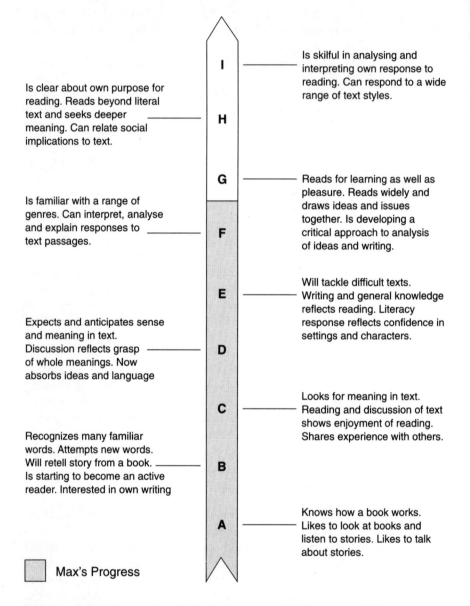

Is skilful in analysing and interpreting own response to reading. Can respond to a wide range of text styles.

Is clear about own purpose for reading. Reads beyond literal text and seeks deeper meaning. Can relate social implications to text.

Reads for learning as well as pleasure. Reads widely and draws ideas and issues together. Is developing a critical approach to analysis of ideas and writing.

Is familiar with a range of genres. Can interpret, analyse and explain responses to text passages.

Will tackle difficult texts. Writing and general knowledge reflects reading. Literacy response reflects confidence in settings and characters.

Expects and anticipates sense and meaning in text. Discussion reflects grasp of whole meanings. Now absorbs ideas and language

Looks for meaning in text. Reading and discussion of text shows enjoyment of reading. Shares experience with others.

Recognizes many familiar words. Attempts new words. Will retell story from a book. Is starting to become an active reader. Interested in own writing

Knows how a book works. Likes to look at books and listen to stories. Likes to talk about stories.

Max's Progress

Max's and the other students' development was far from a stepwise sequence of development. What was to count as reading had been established with the whole group through the use of the *Tell Me* strategy. The large-group discussions were used to scaffold ways to think and talk about texts and ideas. The small-group discussions allowed the students to take control and regulate their own behaviour. The students were learning how to be participants in discussion about books in this classroom as they developed their knowledge of literacy and control of their mental processes. These students realized that they were not passive receptacles of information, but that their minds were active construction agents of meaning. When Max insisted that reading was also talk, he was demonstrating understanding that meaning was socially constructed.

It had been important to use activities which were not substitutes for literary response and pleasure and which did not draw away from literature and the experience of reading. This premise prevented developmental assumptions influencing text choice. Max had been presented with a library from which to develop literary enjoyment and critical skills and allowed to talk. Like all avid readers, the main pleasure of literature for Max became the dialogue it engendered.

Reading development for Max was idiosyncratic and tied to the taking on of ideas from others and transforming them into his own. All of the students were observed following zig-zag paths and the final reading bore little resemblance to what the talk had been about early in the year. Images, patterns, subjective responses and puzzles were ways of describing how understandings from life, and from other texts, influence reading.

Although Max seems to have completed Band F some indicators will probably be able to be inferred. For example, he uses the plots and characters in a novel to make wider meanings, rather than map them out. Undoubtedly he could list the elements of narrative but this would be unproductive. Max has learnt that there are many text worlds to be built during a reading which may in no way resemble the one at the end. Just as in life!

Moderation

Max's teacher wondered if her judgement of Max's progress was too subjective and took her doubts to a moderation meeting with the other grade six teachers. In this school moderation is used as a means of addressing the variations within and between teachers' assessments of students' work. It is the process of bringing individual judgements into line with general standards. The moderation process gives teachers the opportunity to share their interpretation of a student's work. This can be thought of as *reflecting out loud* (Griffin and Nix, 1991).

The teachers in the moderating session used the Nutshell statements from Bands E and F to support their agreement with Max's teacher. These statements may be seen in the rocket figure.

- Band E. Will tackle difficult texts. Writing and general knowledge reflect reading. Literary response reflects confidence in settings and characters.

Figure 7.3 Reading band F. The American literacy profile scales

---

F   **Reading Strategies**
Describes links between personal experience and arguments and ideas about text. Selects relevant passages or phrases to answer questions without necessarily reading the whole text. Formulates research topics and questions and finds relevant information from reading materials. Maps out plots and character development in novels and other literary texts. Varies reading strategies according to purposes for reading and nature of text. Makes connections between texts, recognizing similarities of themes and values.

Responses
Discusses author's intent for the reader. Discusses styles used by different authors. Describes settings in literature. Forms generalizations about a range of genres, including myth, short stories. Offers reasons for the feelings provoked by a text. Writing and discussions acknowledge a range of interpretations of text. Offers critical opinion or analysis of reading passages in discussion. Justifies own appraisal of a text. Synthesizes and expands on information from a range of texts in written work.

• Band F. Is familiar with a range of genres. Can interpret, analyse and explain responses to text passages.

The teachers also talked about how the body of knowledge about what it is to be a reader of literature was being developed. These new indicators could be filled in at the space provided on the profile form to provide rich data about a reader. These teachers had reached consensus very easily in this case. It was also interesting to hear over several days the moderating process carried on informally in staffroom talk.

The literacy profiles

A sample of Max's work and thinking has helped give a sense of Max's lively development as a reader. The literacy profiles allowed for the collection of data about Max's reading when the teaching and learning were taking place. The indicators of development accumulated in an observable fashion as his reading abilities progressively emerged and his knowledge of the reading process expanded. The literacy scale was used by the teacher as a manageable way of rating progress. The indicators are evidently present in his work and they provide a common vocabulary for describing progress.

Literacy profiles enable teachers to embody all the best principles of assessment and reporting practices by encouraging them to use multiple methods of observation and by providing criterion-referenced descriptions.

References

Bakhtin, M. M. (1981) *The Dialogic Imagination: Four Essays,* ed. M. Holquist and trans. C. Emerson, Austin, Texas: University of Texas Press.

Bruner, J. (1986) *Actual Minds Possible Worlds,* Cambridge, MA: Harvard University Press.

Chambers, A. (1993) *Tell Me,* Stroud, England: Thimble Press.

Clay, M. (1979) *Reading: the Patterning of Complex Behaviour,* London: Heinemann.

Clay, M. (1991) 'Developmental learning puzzles me', *Australian Journal of Reading* 14 (4): 263–76.

Goodman, K. (1970) 'Reading: a psycholinguistic guessing game', in H. Singer and R. Ruddell (eds) *Theoretical Models and Processes of Reading,* Newark, DE: International Reading Association.

Goodman, K. (1973) *Miscue Analysis: Applications to Reading Instruction,* Urbana, IL: ERIC Clearinghouse on Reading and Communication Skills.

Goodman, K. (1985) 'Unity in reading', in H. Singer and R. Ruddell, *Theoretical Models and Processes of Reading,* Newark, DE: International Reading Association.

Goodman, K. (1993) Paper presented at First International Conference of the Australian Reading Association, Melbourne, Australia, July.

Griffin, P. E. (1989) 'Monitoring children's growth towards literacy', John Smith Memorial Lecture, University of Melbourne, 5 September, *Bulletin of VIER* (Victoria Institute of Education Research), 61: 45–72.

Griffin, P. E. and Nix, P. (1991) *Educational Assessment and Reporting: A New Approach,* Sydney: Harcourt Brace Jovanovich.

Griffin, P. E., Smith, P. G. and Burrill, L. (1995) *The American Literacy Profile Scales,* Portsmouth, NH: Heinemann.

Harste, J., Short, C. G., and Burke, C. L. (1988) *Creating Classrooms for Authors: The Reading–Writing Connection,* Portsmouth, NH: Heinemann.

Harste, J., Woodward, V. A. and Burke, C. L. (1984) *Language Stories and Literacy Lessons,* Portsmouth, NH: Heinemann.

Rosenblatt, L. M. (1978) *The Reader, the Text, the Poem: the Transactional Theory of Literary Work,* Carbondale, IL: Southern Illinois University Press.

Victoria, Ministry of Education (1988) *The Literacy Profile Scales Handbook.*

Wells, G. (1986) *The Meaning Makers,* London: Hodder & Stoughton.

Children's books

Crew, G. and illus. Rogers, G. (1992) *Lucy's Bay,* Australia: Jam Roll Press.

Knowles, S. and illus. Clement, R. (1988) *Edward the Emu,* Australia: Angus & Robertson.

Macdonald, C. (1993) *The Lake at the End of the World,* Australia: Puffin.

Marsden, J. (1990) *Out of Time,* Australia: Pan Macmillan.

Sutcliff, R. (1956) *The Shield Ring,* London: Oxford University Press.

8

ASSESSING OLDER STUDENTS' RESPONSE TO FICTION

Classroom-based activity to support system-wide assessment

Mike Hamlin

My career as a secondary-school teacher of English began in 1976. This was fortunate, as it meant that my first public examination class coincided with the first *national* extension of a 100 per cent course work (folio-based) form of assessment. This public examination at 16+ was at the end of compulsory schooling for most and was also a gateway for some into further education from 16 to 18 years. This assessment option was offered by the Northern Examinations and Assessment Board based in Manchester and it had already been operating successfully amongst schools in the North of England since 1965.

The Examinations Board responsible for this innovation was aware of the need to convince a range of interested parties that it was possible to use teacher assessment in this way to arrive at valid and reliable grades in high-stakes assessment. The very first report on this experimental form of assessment back in 1965 summarized the problem in this way:

> The examination in English Language is under bitter criticism as conducive to dull and cramped teaching and to crabbed rote learning and practice. The lively interest which should be aroused by learning to read and write English is killed, so it is asserted, by the need to prepare for writing answers to stereotyped questions on English Language papers. (Leeming 1994)

After two years' experience in course work/folio assessment its second report in 1966 concluded: 'It appears that the principal results of the experiment (in folio assessment) have been the encouragement of wider reading, more opportunity to discuss what has been read, freer and wider experiment in writing' (Leeming 1994).

The popularity of this form of assessment grew rapidly in these early years. Accompanying this numerical expansion were important developments in standardization procedures. If course work assessment was to succeed, all parties would need to be convinced by the rigour of its internal standardization procedures. The procedures put in place were these:

1   At the beginning of the school year teachers received *trial marking* materials. These consisted of the photocopied work of four anonymous students. Teachers, individually and in teams, were required to award each candidate a grade on an A to G scale. The results were then to be sent to the Examinations Board.

2   Two months later two departmental representatives attended a local *agreement trial*. This would typically consist of ten or twelve local schools meeting for an afternoon. They had before them a printout showing the grades awarded to the trial marking material by each participating teacher as well as all the departmentally agreed grades. The printout also showed the grade already agreed by the *National Review Panel*. With this information teachers focused their sometimes heated discussions on the work of those candidates where there was the greatest discrepancy between the views of teachers and those of the Review Panel. This whole procedure was repeated in the following school term with a fresh collation of student materials.

3   After two agreement trials schools submitted the work of their own students for 'real' marking. Precise requirements changed over the years but typically, ten assignments were selected for each candidate; these needed to demonstrate a range of materials covered and tasks attempted. A minimum of one task had to be completed under controlled classroom conditions, thereby providing a marker for estimating whether any untoward outside help was being given (in practice this proved very rarely to be a problem).

4   A process of *internal moderation* then began where the assignments and grades of one teacher in the department were compared to others and a final departmental grade agreed. These internally moderated grades were then sent to the Examinations Board where a selection of *sample candidates* representing the entire range would be identified. The work for these sample candidates (fifteen or twenty in number) would then be sent to a nominated *Inter-School Assessor* (ISA). Inter-School Assessors would mark the scripts and award grades on the A to G scale, also without any knowledge of the school's assessment. The grades awarded by the ISA and the school would then be compared by the Board using statistical tests of standards, conformity and discrimination.

5   At the next stage Review Panel members would become involved. Each agreement trial group would be represented by at least one member on the Review Panel. Each member would now receive and moderate

the work of about five schools, but unlike the ISA's, the Review Panel members *would* be notified of the grade awarded to each candidate in a school's sample. They would also be asked to comment on the appropriateness of a school's grades and order of merit via a detailed questionnaire. The considerations of the ISA and the Review Panel member would eventually reach the Examinations Board and decisions would be made as to the nature of the review, if any, which would need to be made of a school's work. At one extreme: a blanket review of all students' work at a school; through specific reviews of grade subdivisions which might be causing concern; down to no need for a review at all. Any adjustments to the grades of a school had to be agreed by Review Panel members and then ratified by a Senior Moderator.

6 Once agreed, the final student grades would be released on a day at the end of the school year (common for all exam boards and for all subjects).

This formidably complex yet democratically accountable structure was to continue, with only marginal changes, for the next seventeen years. In retrospect this represents a huge period of administrative consistency and accumulating professional expertise.

By 1993, across the country as a whole, some 80 per cent of students were being entered for 100 per cent course work examination schemes in English, with only 20 per cent opting for the alternative, more traditional forms of examination (Leeming 1994). This figure of 80 per cent goes some way in explaining the severity of the blow felt by teachers of English when the Conservative Government announced, as part of its controversial and complex National Curriculum proposals, that from 1994 *all* assessment schemes at 16+ would contain a *maximum* weighting of 20 per cent for course work.

Softening the blow?

The decision to limit course work to around 20 per cent of any assessment was a severe blow to the majority of English departments who were successfully using 100 per cent course work schemes. However, the political decision *was* taken, course work *has* been limited (at least for the foreseeable future). So how best to work within these new requirements without reverting to the 'dull and cramped teaching' and the 'crabbed rote learning' referred to earlier? How best to soften this blow?

The six independent Examinations Boards in England were first given the job of developing syllabuses to fit these newly imposed requirements. The relative assessment weightings, however, were common *and* mandatory:

20 per cent	*Speaking and listening* activities (teacher assessed)
20 per cent	*Course work* submission, of which
	10 per cent for reading activities (teacher assessed)
	10 per cent for writing activities (teacher assessed)
60 per cent	*Final examination*, of which
	30 per cent for reading tasks
	30 per cent for writing tasks.

The solution the Northern Board presented for the first of the new-style examinations in 1994 included some novel interpretations. First, there was a desire to provide a syllabus which would facilitate the integration of the study of English into a unified course for candidates also taking English Literature. Second, there was an attempt to keep the limited amount of course work as structurally central as possible. Third, there was an attempt to use pre-released material in new and significant ways (NEAB 1994–7).

The full details of the alternatives available are complex but some of the distinguishing features include:

Oral course work (20 per cent)

At suitable points in the course, the teacher would undertake and record an assessment of oral evidence for speaking and listening. The record should include a list of the oral activities undertaken.

Written course work (20 per cent)

Typically, five or six assignments. In planning and setting course work it is stressed that the key to both coherence and success lies in the creation of meaningful and relevant contexts for speaking and listening, reading and writing and, hence, effective links between them. Schools are also encouraged to use course work to prepare candidates for the demands of the Terminal Examination.

Terminal examination (60 per cent)

Paper 1 – A two-hour examination in two sections, which is common to both English and English Literature. *Section A* requires responses to the close reading of a Board-set Anthology of prepared texts. This Anthology to consist of short whole texts and extracts from longer texts to be distributed free to centres, early in the term prior to that of the examination. Each candidate to have their own copy of the Anthology and the texts used will cover a range of genres and periods and will include some Shakespeare. *Section B* requires responses to the close reading of unseen texts. Short whole texts and/or extracts from a range of genres and periods would be presented to candidates along with a series of structured questions.

Paper 2 (English) – A two-hour examination in two sections. *Section A* requires candidates to understand, order and present facts, ideas and opinions, using a variety of stimulus materials (for some of the syllabus alternatives this stimulus material can be pre-released to schools). *Section B* requires candidates to write imaginatively in response to appropriate stimulus materials.

Paper 2 (English Literature) – A two hour paper organized into five sections, each relating to one of the prescribed Area of Study as set out in the syllabus (Images of War, Myth and Symbolism, Experiences of School, etc.). Candidates are required to answer questions on *two* texts, each from a different Area of Study. The texts studied are allowed to be taken into the examination room; in this sense it can be characterized as an *open-book* examination.

Working with a pre-released examination Anthology in a mixed ability classroom

The theme for the Northern Board's 1995 Anthology was *People and Environment*. It contained a total of fifteen texts comprising two complete short stories, seven poems, three of which were pre-twentieth century, three drama extracts, including an extract from Shakespeare, and three prose extracts, one of which was pre-twentieth century.

The Anthologies arrived in January and the examination was not until early June. We decided that we would begin work on the Anthology at the end of March and allow for approximately five weeks of intensive study. Given the Easter break, this would still permit three or four weeks of final preparation before the exams began in earnest.

We also knew the areas we needed to cover. There would be three questions in all, one would focus exclusively on the lead short story, 'The Oakum Room' by Theresa Tomlinson; one would focus on the *language aspects* of at least two of the Anthology texts of our own choosing, the final question would concentrate on the way in which links had been made between people and their environments in two further texts, which again, we could nominate.

Where to begin? Since the Anthologies were to be distributed one per student and they would each retain their own copy right up until the examination, there was only one opportunity for any surprise tactics – that is, right at the beginning before any of the copies had been allocated. We decided that the first text we would approach would be a pre-twentieth century prose extract, in this case the opening extract from *Great Expectations* by Charles Dickens, where Pip first encounters the terrifying stranger in the churchyard. Although relatively well known, none of my class had read the text as part of their general reading.

I began by holding back the Anthology proper and photocopying only the first paragraph of the extract, which I distributed without any contextualization at all. I suggested to the class that, working in pairs, they closely read this mini-extract several times, jotting down which words and phrases told them something about *the character* of Pip, and which suggested something about *when* the action might be taking place.

This activity was then repeated for the second paragraph, which was distributed in the same way, with the same paired task. Paragraph three allowed a further dimension to be introduced, by asking for evidence as to *where* this action might be taking place and whether the material contained in this paragraph might now persuade them to change their minds regarding their earlier conclusions from paragraphs one and two.

Next, pulling together insights from the previous tasks, the groups were asked to nominate what *sort of story* they thought this might be from, and what might happen next, by producing a short list of story possibilities.

One student pair made the following notes for these three tasks:

Task One – People and Time – Pip must be an orphan, he has no mother or father, they died when he was very young, and he remembers nothing of them. 'My first fancies regarding what they were like, were unreasonably derived by their tombstones'. Pip does not have a high opinion of his brothers as they chose 'to give up trying to find a living'. He seems a little simple as he called himself Pip because he couldn't say his full name Philip Pirrip.

It all took place early in his life as he speaks of his 'childish conclusions', but he is thinking about his past and he could now be in his middle life and remembering little bits about himself when he was young.

Task Two – Time and Place – It's a country place with fields and hills, not much life apart from cattle. It's a place which lies by the sea. A very quiet place 'this bleak place overgrown with nettles was a churchyard'. It was 'intersected with dykes and mounds and gates with scattered cattle feeding on it, was the marshes'. These are good descriptions which show a country life with nothing but grass, little to do. As Pip discovers things about his surroundings he seems afraid of what he has found and what he learns about his family, he is a frightened child.

Task Three – Story Predictions – The story is about the life of a child, the writer perhaps being that child, thinking about his past, his experiences and how he grew up. It has a sadness about it, how he found life and what he thought about it.

The child might go on to find out about his parents and how they died, he might find other family members to help him in his quest. It might move on to other experiences in his life, being a teenager then a man, how he deals with his experiences, how they make him feel.

At this point I distributed the Anthologies and we all turned to this particular text. We found that it was from *Great Expectations* by Charles Dickens and this either confirmed or disturbed some of the interim conclusions the group had been drawing together. As a well-known pre-twentieth-century text, it also provides more evidence around the style of language used in the extract.

We now read to the end of the extract, through the meeting with the frightening stranger, up until the point where Pip runs home without stopping. The group were then given the task of constructing four questions which best made sense of the passage as a whole, and which were to include one creative, write-on type of question.

One pair generated the following questions before going on to develop their answers :

> What can we say about the man in the churchyard from the way he is described?
> What type of boy was Pip? How did he react to the man?
> Now that we know Charles Dickens wrote this piece, does it make any difference to what *we* feel about it?
> Pip runs home to his sister's house, what would he say to her? Would he tell the truth?

This strikes me as being a pretty comprehensive exploration of this particular text. I attempted to provide an initial framework around which the students could work, and through a structured series of individual tasks and shared response, gradually pulled back to allow the students to devise their own routes through this potentially challenging piece. Working steadily, these activities comfortably filled the two double and one single lessons which we have as English time each week.

By now we all had copies of the Anthology and I felt it important to introduce an element of student choice into which texts we would go on to examine. I first explained the three types of question that we were likely to encounter in the final examination. We had already considered one pre-twentieth century text which had given us plenty of sensible things to say on the way language provides clues about people, places and times. Perhaps we should now consider an extract which might work as a complete contrast to the Dickens extract.

After a period of browsing, we discussed the problem again and decided that the drama extract from *Easy on the Relish* by Andrew Bethell might fit the bill as a suitably effective contrast to Dickens. The extract is set in Binders, an American hamburger chain about to open a new branch in London. Claud Tofler, a recent graduate of the 'Hamburger University', is the manager. He employs a mixed bunch of young Londoners, from many different cultural backgrounds. The extract begins with Tofler about to deliver an introductory 'pep' talk to his new recruits.

Our focus for exploration was the language used by Tofler, a kind of American psycho-babble. This contemporary usage contrasted well with the period style of the Dickens extract. The drama text also provided obvious possibilities for group work and improvisations because of the variety of roles presented and their sometimes reluctant relationship with their working environment. After a lot of enactment and evaluation it was decided that our main written task would be to write and perform Tofler's final motivating speech on the morning of the burger bar's grand opening.

One student produced the following script:

> 8:45am Binders Burger Bar, Saturday morning. Binders is due to open for the first time in just fifteen minutes.
> (Tofler stands on a stool and claps his hands for order)
> Tofler : Okey Dokey ! Okey Dokey!
> Come on now a little bit of hush please.
> (Claps hands again).
> I sure hope y'all rough 'n ready and rarin' to show those hamburger gobblin', malt slurpin', fry munchin' customers out there that Binders is the place to be.
> Y'all got your instruction pack and your itemised work schedules, so you should all know exactly what you're doin'.
> (Slight sound of shuffling and murmurs from the workforce)
> Come on, come on. Where's those Binders' smiles?
> Let's take it from the top okay ?
> Binders, Binders, we're the best
> We make burgers beat the . . . .
> (No-one joins in)
> Come on now, . . . please!
> Where are those smiles?
> I don't know Merle,
> Thursday you forgot your hat,
> today it's your smile
> All of you now, en-thu-si-asm.
> That's what needs to be pumping around your bodies.

Smiles, enthusiasm.
Let's do it once more
Binders, Binders, we're the best. . . .
(The rest join in, droning on unenthusiastically)

We had now focused on one prose and a drama extract, as a group we decided to move on by examining two contrasting poems from the Anthology. After much browsing and discussion we agreed on 'Old Woman' by Elizabeth Jennings (for the links between a complex older character and her home setting), and 'Me Aunty Connie' by Terry Lee (for its use of colloquial language and its alternative focus on a woman's working environment).

'Old Woman' – After an initial group brainstorming of links between the character of the older woman and the specifics of her home environment, we agreed that our task should be the construction of an emotional *time-line* taking this woman through the significant stages of her life as they are expressed in the poem. Working pairs were expected to argue for the appropriateness of their own time-lines. The time-line linked the following events:

1   Meets husband, love grows, they marry.
2   Life before children, easy going, timeless, relaxed.
3   Has children, involved in organizing their lives.
4   One by one, children grow up and leave home.
5   Second life together with husband, growing older, involved but calmer.
6   Death of husband, now alone with memories.
7   No longer cares about time, at one with her possessions, memories and mementoes.

'Me Aunty Connie' – Here the initial focus was language, specifically the colloquial, conversational style used by the poet to describe her Aunty Connie. We then moved on to consider some of the ways people make sense of their working lives.

Me Aunty worked at Carson's,
On the cream button.
She put the dollop on the cake
As it passed along the conveyor belt.
She'd been there fifteen years.
                                        Terry Lee

The poem ends with Aunty Connie being dismissed for dolloping the wrong cakes!

Most of the group immediately wanted to follow her fortunes, with a similar piece of writing describing the job she might move on to after working for so long at Carson's cake factory. One student wrote:

Me Aunty does the food
Down at Pork Farms Caff.
She spreads the bread with marge.
She makes the Yorkshire pud.

The foreman is me Uncle Bob.
She sneaks him extra eggs.
She gets to wear a hair-net,
And a pinny, with a badge.

She works with a woman,
Who used to work with her before.
And they talk about the old days,
Down at Carsons.

The fifth and final text to be studied was the short story – 'The Oakum Room'. As the lead short story, we knew that a question would be directed specifically at this text. So we decided to organize our detailed notes around two distinct organizing concepts – *Descriptions* and *Motivations*: *What* was the workhouse and its officers really like? *Why* did the women inmates behave in the way they did?

Discussion on these two aspects led on to attempts to reconstruct the atmosphere of the workhouse in the classroom, and to improvise around some of the events described in the story.

In all, five texts were studied in some detail. The nature and timing of the pre-released materials made it possible for me to plan some initial ways into the Anthology and to ensure that the group as a whole was able to decide on which particular texts would be explored using which strategies – without ever losing sight of the final examination requirements. I suggest that this level of student engagement would not have been possible had the terminal examination restricted itself to unseen passages for student analysis and discussion.

What the students thought about this way of working

As the work on the examination Anthology was coming to an end, we were lucky in having two student teachers available to carry out a research project, part of which was to 'Explore and document new approaches to assessing reading and response to reading'. In particular, the student teachers were able to interview a number of pupils concerning their thoughts on the Anthology activities they had just undertaken.

The pupils were interviewed in some depth, in an attempt to assess the effectiveness of the particular classroom strategies employed by the teacher. There was also some opportunity for the student teachers to discuss with the pupils their reading experiences during other parts of the English course as well as their personal reading habits. Their interim research conclusions were both interesting and helpful.

All the pupils responded well to the *Great Expectations* extract from the Anthology. Pupils recollected the predictions made in class and remembered their enjoyment of this particular teaching strategy. Pupils had enjoyed working in pairs and discussing their prediction with others. Pupils recollected that in group or paired discussion they were sharing their opinions with others, hearing other opinions which were similar to and thus confirming of their own ideas, or, on hearing different opinions, they were able to change their minds and acquire fresh insights regarding the extract.

Most of the pupils, in discussing the *Great Expectations* extract, referred to the old fashioned language used in the piece and contrasted this with their own personal use of language. Others referred to the sense of atmosphere created in the piece and were able to closely refer to the extract, often remembering particular words or phrases in order to support their ideas. (The theme for the Anthology was *People and Environment*, and the pupils had evidently remembered specific details about the environment created in this extract.)

Pupils particularly remembered the character of the 'stranger' in the extract, who was often referred to as a tramp or a pirate. Some of the pupils obviously had a definite picture in their heads as to how this character would look. They also clearly remembered his behaviour towards Pip and Pip's reaction to this.

Several of the pupils offered comments on *Easy on the Relish*. In particular, pupils had enjoyed reading this in the classroom. The strategy employed for this extract was that pupils were asked to take on the roles in the drama extract and then to perform these roles to the group. Pupils found it easy to understand this piece, and several references were made to the fact that it was based in the present day and in a burger bar that pupils were familiar with. The pupils considered the language of the piece easy to understand.

They also recalled the use of American English in the piece, and referred to the fact that this created a strong image of the type of person Claud Tofler might be like, i.e. like a baseball coach! They were also aware of the fact that this use of American English by Tofler may not be effective or even appropriate in Britain, as he was obviously not achieving the required results with his staff.

A smaller number of the students interviewed expressed their enjoyment or understanding of the poetry from the Anthology. One student had enjoyed 'Old Woman' and he referred to the fact that on an initial reading he had not been particularly impressed with the poem but working it through in pairs, he began to see more meaning in the piece.

In discussing other aspects of their course, pupils recalled *An Inspector Calls* with some pleasure, in particular, referring to the fact that the play was read in class with pupils taking on the various roles. Pupils were able to remember the plot, and recalled the atmosphere of suspense created by the writer, J. B. Priestley. Pupils thought that taking on roles helped them to understand the different characters in the play.

When discussing their personal reading habits, all of the pupils commented that they had far less time for reading for their own enjoyment. This was due to the amount of time that they had to devote to reading and revising examination material. Some of the pupils expressed regret at this, though a few still managed to set aside some time for their own reading, albeit less than they would like.

What examiners thought about the performance of candidates on pre-released as opposed to unseen materials

An interview with an examiner who had marked five hundred examination scripts for the Northern Board suggested that schools differed widely in the ways in which they approached the pre-released materials. Some schools saw the opportunities for a more sustained student engagement with the assessment materials as being helpful in the creation of independent, critical readers, able to comment widely on the texts; others used the time to weigh students down with prepackaged responses which tended to limit their role as autonomous respondees.

> At best, candidates would approach the Anthology questions with confidence and independence. They obviously had a lot to say; they knew their own ways around the texts and were able to draw out a series of complex inferences and comparisons.
>
> At worst, candidates would attempt to repeat strings of points and priorities culled from half remembered handouts from their teachers. With these candidates a kind of literary train-spotting was operating, where every incidence of alliteration, simile or metaphor would be obsessively identified and commented upon. (Watkinson 1995)

Predictably perhaps, given the huge switch from 100 per cent course work to 60 per cent terminal examinations, an 'exam fever' gripped some teachers and as a consequence they tended to over-teach, over-direct and thus limit the scope for autonomous student engagement with the pre-released texts.

The centres that managed to strike a more balanced approach, however, did prepare students in ways which would have been impossible had unseen texts been the only examination focus. Students from these centres were able to range confidently across the texts, making connections which made powerful sense to them, as young, engaged readers. Ironically, with some of these candidates this textual confidence spilt over into the *unseen* section where several were able to make telling points, comparing aspects of the unseen materials with equivalents from the pre-released Anthology.

Changing practice

As for the future, one major Examinations Board is already proposing an extended role for pre-released examination materials in English and English Literature, and others are likely to follow suit. Given these developments it becomes even more important for schools and colleges to develop strategies which enable students to engage independently with the texts offered and which *link positively* with other forms of assessment – whether through course work submission, open-book forms of literary assessment or even variants of unseen response.

The need for professional development in this area is obvious. At the moment, critics are able to point to the use of pre-released materials for assessment purposes and warn that they make students vulnerable to teacher limitations, that low teacher expectations or expertise place a ceiling on student achievement and that nationally imposed 'tests' may not. (Of course, this point is made even more strongly when attacking forms of course work submission.)

Clearly, not all teachers are skilled at setting enabling tasks, not all teachers fully understand how their own assumptions about the nature of the subject or about the expectations of 'the Examining Board' may impose limits on student performance. But the answer, surely, lies in making use of the many opportunities pre-released materials (and course work folios) provide for effective in-service training at the departmental, regional and national level, as well as recognizing the changing ways in which teachers can access the professional support they need.

It is not claimed that the approaches suggested in this chapter are original but they do have the advantage of being informed by some of the new ways of thinking about assessing response to reading. The approach outlined here is part of the debate around appropriate teaching and learning strategies which have the aim of optimizing student reading response within a high-stakes examination system. Such debate needs to continue.

References

Leeming, D. (1994) *A Report on Coursework Examinations in English and English Literature,* Northern Examinations and Assessment Board.

Northern Examinations and Assessment Board (1994–97) *Syllabuses for English and English Literature GCSE Examinations.*

Watkinson (1995) Author interview with R. Watkinson, NEAB Examiner.

9

READING WHILE WRITING

An approach to the assessment of reading through discussions of the drafting process

Alan Dewar

This chapter sets out to see if useful information about pupils' reading can be gained from interviewing them about drafts of their own writing. It examines taped interviews with three pupils and describes the kind of information which is generated by those interviews. It then discusses the value and purposes of such information, and the relationships between information gained in this way and the other kinds of information we can gather about pupils' reading.

The starting point of this exploration is the recognition that, although reading and writing are often separated for assessment purposes, in practice they are so closely related as to be almost inseparable. Most syllabuses and schemes of work assume that reading and writing will go on together, and their assessment, even when reported separately, is mutually dependent. This is a point made in detail in the chapter by Harrison, Bailey and Foster in this volume. The approach I describe accepts the inaccessibility of the reading process as far as assessment is concerned, and gathers information about reading by inference from what pupils say about the changes they have made to their own texts.

Reading while writing

When pupils compose, and when they make changes to their writing during the process of composition, they are making decisions and solving problems. Flower (1981) gives an account of writing as a problem-solving procedure, in which she describes the decisions made by writers as 'using rules', 'using trial and error' and 'using heuristics'. While each of these is a strategy for *producing* texts, in order to make decisions about *changing* texts – to become aware of the rhetorical problems which result in changes to texts – the pupils need to read their own work critically. Only then can they devise rhetorical strategies to overcome the problems they identify during their critical reading.

This seems like a grand formula to describe an everyday occurrence, but I think it is important to acknowledge the sophistication of the language skills which are needed to redraft written work. While an understanding of what goes on during the drafting process has been developing among cognitive psychologists, administrators of education have not paid that process much systematic attention. For example, Bereiter and Scardamalia (1987) offer wonderfully complex psychological models of writing: good for understanding what goes on during the process of composition; bad for formulating educational policy. Consequently the acknowledgement that drafting is a vital process in composition is not often met with either a curriculum or an assessment procedure which embodies that acknowledgement.

To take the example I know best, the national system of assessment in England separates reading from writing, identifying them as different 'attainment targets' requiring independent test scores and teacher assessments. The programmes of study which accompany this assessment system preserve this separation while acknowledging that 'pupils' abilities should be developed within an integrated programme of speaking and listening, reading and writing' (DFE 1995: 4, repeated on 11 and 17).

The descriptions of expected performance specify that 'critical responses' to texts will be a characteristic of responses to reading only at higher ranges of ability in the later stages of secondary education (14–16-year-olds). However, the English National Curriculum also states that during primary school, when pupils are between 7 and 11 years of age, they 'should be given opportunities to plan, draft and improve their work on paper and on screen, and to discuss and evaluate their own and others' writing' (DFE 1995: 15).

As I have noted, it is difficult to see how changes to a pupil's own writing during the drafting process can be made without some kind of 'critical response'. The separation of reading from writing here gives rise to what appears to be an anomaly: that pupils need 'higher order' reading skills to be able to perform fairly rudimentary writing tasks. Rosenblatt (1994) illustrates some of the inter-relatedness of reading and writing:

> The writer, it is generally recognized, is the first reader of the text. Note an obvious, though neglected, difference: while readers transact with a writer's finished text, writers first read the text as it is being inscribed. Since both reading and writing are recursive processes carried on over a period of time, their very real similarities have masked a basic difference. The writer will often reread the total finished text, but, perhaps more important, the

writer first reads, carries on a spiral, transactional relationship with the very text emerging on the page. (p. 175)

The failure of the National Curriculum in England to recognize the need for such critical responses in a 'spiral, transactional relationship' even in the earliest stages of drafting is unnecessarily limiting, serving the needs of a hierarchy of qualities rather than accurately describing the acquisition of language skills and strategies. The national system in this respect is not helpful to teachers and pupils who are working to develop the complex interaction between reading and writing which goes on in classrooms. The effect of such unrealistic schemes on the practice of teachers has not yet been assessed, but it seems reasonable at least to draw attention to the lack of realism.

Teachers in Britain do give attention to drafting and I would suggest that such attention can be paid in two fairly distinct ways: as a process of correcting technical errors and producing 'fair copies', and as a means of revising texts. I have yet to read any descriptions which establish the relative frequency of these two possible approaches. When teachers and pupils are giving their attention to the revision of texts, there is a sharp focus on audience, with the writer being invited to consider the reader in a variety of ways. The writing conference is also a fairly common way of alerting the writer to inconsistencies, obscurities, opportunities and so on. The revision which takes place in all cases must rely on some interactions between reading and writing skill: most revisions, I should guess, take place without a conference, and revision is not simply a process of the writer being obedient to the recommendations of an audience.

In considering what can be learned about pupils' reading from what they say about their own process of composition, I am also raising a corollary question – 'what reading skills *are* needed in order to undertake any process of revision?' – but that is a question which I do not tackle directly in this chapter.

Talking about reading-while-writing

These interviews were conducted with 13–14-year-old pupils by a visiting teacher and were focused on a sequence of work which had been designed to draw attention, over an extended period, to the possible stages of the drafting process.

The class had been given a series of homework activities which allowed them – or in some cases obliged them – to attend to some highlighted components of the process of composition. The pupils were asked to write a story called 'The Quest'. It could be set anywhere, at any time in history, or in an imaginary time and place, but had the following pre-determined plot:

1   something or someone important is lost;
2   someone sets out to find it or them;
3   difficulties are encountered;
4   the missing object or person is recovered.

Each homework had an introduction in class. At various points there were in-class conferences with peers, and each homework had a teacher response in writing, sometimes consisting of detailed suggestion, sometimes simply of a few words of encouragement.

The pupils' attention was drawn to processes focused, in a somewhat artificial sequence, on pre-drafting, plotting, character development, setting and atmosphere, the opening, revision after conferences, 'cutting and pasting', climax, resolution and proofreading.

In the following extract, the visiting teacher is asking Chloe about the changes she has made to her story.

Chloe: Well, I changed little bits now and again, like the speeches that they said, I'd turn the words round. And the things that they did.
Teacher: Why? Why do you think you changed those bits?
Chloe: Because the way that I'd wrote it ... in some people's eyes it didn't sound right or look right.
Teacher: Why some people's eyes? Who do you mean?
Chloe: 'Cos like ... er ... people who read it like me mum and my friends. Some people says, 'I don't like the sound of this bit, I think you should change it.'
Teacher: Right, and even if. ... Did you agree with everything they said?
Chloe: No, I agreed with bits that they said.
Teacher: So ...what, you just changed those bits you agreed with?
Chloe: Yeah, yeah.

The judgements Chloe is making are naïve in some respects, sophisticated in others, and for a teacher to work with her to develop those judgements would involve detailed and reciprocal understandings. Such understandings are informed by interview data in ways that are not reducible. Some of that complexity is apparent in the way Chloe uses the reactions of her mother and her friends, who form both a real and an internalized audience for her work.

Chloe: Sometimes if I'd read it two or three times, and then I read it again and something sounded difficult in it, then I'd change it.
Teacher: How did you know what sounded difficult?
Chloe: Like ... er ... some parts, people were doing things I found it like difficult for them to get from one place to another in

a very short time so I had to put some speeches in between
that. . . .

Teacher: What did you look for, what made you sort of look at a specific
piece and say that is right or that is wrong?

Chloe: Well, I had to look for bits where, where I found things difficult. If I found things difficult then I had to look and place
myself in that story. 'Cos I'd been told that I'd got a wide imagination. So if I just think about it a bit and then I can get to
these places.

Teacher: You say difficult. What do you mean by difficult?

Chloe: By difficult is, where things don't sound right, and where things
sound to me as though it's impossible.

Elsewhere in her interview, Chloe refers to real life sources for her characters, to adapting specific techniques from earlier stories of her own and
to reading Roald Dahl and Charles Dickens. (Dahl is her favourite because
'he is a very imaginative person'.) She has a clear set of criteria for her
reading as well as her writing: referring to her own story, she says:

Chloe: I found some of it very boring so I just put – took them out,
and just put it all back together.

Teacher: How do you know they were boring?

Chloe: Because they was boring for me, and I want a person like to
pick up my story and just carry on reading it. And not find it
boring and then putting it down.

Teacher: What makes a story boring for you?

Chloe: If it goes on and on about a certain thing. And it says things
twice.

Teacher: Where have you recognized these boring stories before then?

Chloe: In books that I read.

It is possible to infer quite a lot about Chloe's reading from the interview as a whole. She tends to value character and plot, and is inclined to
regard detail of setting and atmosphere as of lesser importance. (At one
point, she defines the 'unimportant' in storytelling as writing about 'pictures
that people have on walls and that'.) She has a strong sense of stories as
representing real people in real time, even to the point of inventing speeches
to let characters get from one place to another rather than using a narrative intervention – a playwright's technique, rather than a novelist's. She
enjoys a pacy read, and is aware of some devices for promoting pace in
fiction.

Chloe's drafts can be seen alongside the interview as points of reference;
evidence of reading having taken place, of reading strategies having been
in use in conjunction with writing strategies. These inferences can readily

form part of a continuing teaching/learning conversation which has little to do with grades or accountable standards. The information is also difficult to separate out as wholly *reading* assessment; it is entangled with other information – some social, some psychological, some to do with other aspects of language – and is troublesome to the notion of an independent reading 'score'.

If the purpose of conducting the interview is to accelerate the pupil's progress, the information specifically about reading does not need to be disentangled from the accompanying information: that is only necessary when it has to be separately reported. Indeed, it could be argued that such information is meaningful and useable only in its context.

The interviews in this chapter are about pupils' self-assessment as *writers*, but their self-assessments depend upon their abilities as readers. The interviews are concerned with how young writers assess their own writing in the light of what they have read and viewed; of what they know about the world; of what they understand about the principles of assessment by which they believe their work is judged. Their self-assessments are not made for reporting, but for practical purposes.

Interviews overtly represent real people in ways which other forms of assessment information do not. There are some advantages to developing such avowedly subjective information. Russell was interviewed by the same visiting teacher and although it forms only a small part of what we might know about both pupils, there are strong elements of 'portraiture' even in short extracts from the interview.

Teacher: Did you change your story at all?
Russell: Yes.
Teacher: Why did you change it?
Russell: 'Cos, when I was writing it down on the computer I seen bits what I could add on to or take away to make it better.
Teacher: How did you know they made it better?
Russell: Erm, it makes it longer and puts more ... I don't know what to say. It puts more feeling into it.
Teacher: More feeling?
Russell: Yes.
Teacher: Is that the only reason you changed things?
Russell: Yes.
Teacher: Nothing else at all?
Russell: I took some bits away because it didn't sound right.
Teacher: How do you mean it didn't sound right? Why didn't it sound right?
Russell: Erm, well, a bit of it says 'Come back you damn mutt' and stuff like that and it had some more words on the end that didn't sound right.

Teacher: Erm, can you give me a more specific reason why it didn't sound right?
Russell: No. It didn't sound right.
Teacher: Just didn't sound right.
Russell: No.
Teacher: What did you like about your story?
Russell: The way that they got them back from the dog catchers.
Teacher: Yes?
Russell: And they ended up happy.
Teacher: Right. Anything you didn't like about your story?
Russell: No. . . .
Teacher: Do you think you improved your story?
Russell: Not a lot.
Teacher: Not a lot?
Russell: No.
Teacher: Even, maybe a little bit?
Russell: I, I did a little bit, yes.
Teacher: How do you think you improved it a little bit?
Russell: By putting more character into it.
Teacher: More character?
Russell: Yes.
Teacher: Is character important, then?
Russell: Yes.
Teacher: Why?
Russell: If you put character into the people, characters in the story, and people get to read it more, get into it more. . . .
Teacher: Did you think your story improved as you wrote it, or after you finished it?
Russell: No.
Teacher: You don't think it improved. Why not?
Russell: 'Cos, I don't think it did.
Teacher: Any reasons?
Russell: No.
Teacher: Right, why do you think then, it didn't improve?
Russell: Err, don't know.
Teacher: Do you often draft work?
Russell: Yeah.
Teacher: Yes, what effect do you think drafting work has on you, on your writing?
Russell: No idea.
Teacher: No idea, right. Why do you often draft work?
Russell: Because when you draft it you can get it checked by someone to get all the spelling right. But then if you don't draft it and

just write it up on the computer straight on to A4 you might have a lot of spelling mistakes on it.

Even allowing for Russell's laconic suspicion of an unfamiliar interviewer, it is clear that there are several self-assessment processes at work. Russell is aware of possibilities for developing character and feeling in his writing and although his resources for doing so are limited he does have a sense of his readership. He has ideas about a satisfactory ending, perhaps a rather cynical view about the use of detail to make a story 'longer' and some interesting thoughts about the appropriateness of certain kinds of language. That sense of appropriateness leads to redrafts in a couple of places which may impoverish the story's language: 'you damn mutt' is a piece of quite strong characterizing dialogue which is weakened in subsequent drafts, and there is a heavily scored-out word which he has replaced with 'kissing' – presumably a sign of experimentation, or subversion, which he has censored in deference to (accurate) assumptions about what is allowable. (Russell's *written* summative self-assessments throughout years 7–9 are uniformly glum or defensive, and he feels considerable despair in the face of public examination.)

Russell's sense of the purpose of drafting is most strongly influenced by the perception that it is largely a secretarial matter. He is quite resistant to questioning about compositional changes, but is – for Russell – effusive about getting spelling right, even though this is seen as something he can get someone else to do.

Russell's sense of his own work *as a reader* is powerfully conditioned by the criteria of evaluation which he believes are applicable. Pupils' self-assessments cannot be norm-referenced; cannot be used to place them in a rank order or to award a grade. However, 'public' norms, whatever their validity, however accurately perceived, will have a profound influence on a pupil, and that influence might be encouraging or discouraging. Russell's evident discomfort in the face of questions which invite self-assessment could be interpreted as both unfamiliarity with the process and reluctance to express his view of the story. Assessments which seek to build confidence and skill could help to offset those multiplications of disadvantage and could place emphasis on pupils' potential for improvement rather than their sense of failure.

Further, the element of 'portraiture' which is visibly present in self-assessment data helps to alter the purport of the assessment. Although, as we have noted, some form of ad hoc norm-referencing will necessarily be a part of this process, a different approach to assessment can create a broader – and perhaps more humane – context, within which all forms of assessment information can find their place. I would argue that this is a more appropriate context for such information.

In exploring the value of self-assessment, the most obvious concern in this case would be that Russell would not only have less evidence on which to draw than Chloe, but that he would be less able to draw on it, or to recognize it as evidence. If differing ability to read re-establishes itself as differing ability to self-assess, then disadvantage is simply working itself out in another arena. However, it is not necessarily the case that reading abilities and self-assessment abilities are congruent or mutually dependent. Clearly, a commitment to make transparent the criteria and processes of assessment is necessary on the part of the teacher: a difficult task, especially when the criteria are suspect.

Some of these concerns can be seen even more sharply if we consider extracts from an interview with a third pupil, Gemma.

Teacher: Why do you enjoy writing stories?
Gemma: I don't know. I've always had a pretty good imagination. It just gives me the chance to let my imagination run wild.
Teacher: Anything else?
Gemma: I'm good at it. It's one of the things I'm good at.

Is this arrogance, unwarranted confidence, or accurate, secure self-assessment? It is possible to imagine pupils of almost any ability making this assertion. A more coherent picture is formed as the interview continues and the context of Gemma's assertion begins to emerge.

Teacher: Why did you change [your story]?
Gemma: I don't know. I just didn't think it sounded right, some of the things I'd put in and then I'd like strayed a bit and I couldn't get back into the pattern again. So I thought no, I can't put that, and crossed it out.

Gemma's sense of 'pattern' is one she returns to during her interview, and is related both to her own planning and to a recognition of genre characteristics.

Teacher: Why did you choose to write about this particular subject?
Gemma: Err, I don't know, I just thought we've got to do something called 'The Quest', so I just like thought something to do with, something questy . . . they always have to sort of get something, or do something, so I thought, oh yeah, base it round that and see how you go.

She speaks elsewhere in the interview about a fairly extensive reading of fantasy, and here she reveals, rather than claims, the beginnings of an analytic understanding. Part of the attempt to negotiate assessment evidence

with the pupil would need to involve the teacher pointing out such inferences – empowering the pupil doubly by helping them to recognize how
we 'read' their performance and by encouraging them to produce data
which are 'legible' in that sense.

It is easy to see why this kind of reading activity, although quite visible
and necessary in the classroom, is not readily perceived by a national system
of assessment. When reading is embedded so thoroughly in other language
processes, the illusion that it can be independently assessed is hard to maintain. The extracts presented here are focused on reading activities, but the
primary purpose of these activities is not assessment. Rather, the interviews
permit an assessment 'take' on an activity which engages the pupils' real
motives for reading.

In these extracts, Gemma is explaining some of the relationships between
her initial planning and the eventual outcomes in her story.

Teacher: . . . did you refer back to your notes or did the story just come
as you went along, which would you –
Gemma: Most of it just came as I went along.
Teacher: Right.
Gemma: Err, I did look back to see what I'd put in the flowchart and I
thought well let's not stray from the formula too much. So
I just kept looking back and then seeing how I could put
what came into my mind and what was on the flowchart
together.

Gemma's notion of not straying from the formula opens up the possibility
of discussion of the relationships between plot, structure and narrative
texture. It is difficult to see how an analytic approach to an already-composed
text could have done so; more difficult still to devise a comprehension exercise which would access this area of understanding. Similarly, Gemma's
motives for changing one word in the next extract show an awareness which
would be difficult to count toward the award of a score of any kind.

Teacher: Why did you change [this part of the story]?
Gemma: Just to make it a bit more exciting. Some of, some of the things
I'd put, they were sort of dull and I thought that if I put these
words in it they would make it sound more interesting. Instead
of like some others.
Teacher: Right. For instance, if I look at this one here, look. 'Shantra
raised her head to look at her son.' And when it comes to the
final draft you've got the word 'only' son. You've included the
word 'only'.
Gemma: Yeah.
Teacher: Why did you do that?

Gemma: Just to put more emphasis on it. I mean . . . if you was like going to do something then it had to be like, he meant a lot to Shantra, and er, if anything happened to him, she would probably be like, really upset and on her own.

The sensitivity to detail which Gemma is showing here could perhaps be shown by a comprehension exercise, but it would be counter-productive to try to devise tests which would recognize the constellation of small glimpses, guesses, experiments, reading experiences, life experiences, hunches, rules of thumb, blind alleys and so on which make up her sensitivity.

I have suggested that interviews like these can form a basis for exploration of the transactions which form readers' responses, allowing a close connection with active reading strategies and with reading as a process. In practice, pupils in these interviews show evidence of a hotchpotch of reading strategies being applied at need to their drafting. When pupils engage with the drafting process, their attentions seem to focus simultaneously on secretarial errors and on errors or opportunities in composition. There is no suggestion of specific, watertight proofreading or composition read-throughs: they continue to correct continuity errors, to 'improve' character and atmosphere; they continue to tinker every time they return to a text. In other words, their redrafting is not systematic or sequential, in spite of the homework assignment's predisposition towards system and sequence.

Although the initial process of composition is often based on exploration of real-life characters and experiences, it also draws on prior reading and viewing. During redrafting, while there is still an attempt to register accurately the tenor of experience, much of the decision-making about changes to the text seems to be on a holistic basis, governed apparently by reading or viewing preferences. The analyses which are taking place are not clear-cut or explicit; they are part of an attempt to recreate or adapt favoured reading or viewing experiences.

Gemma, unlike Russell, shows a combination of dependence on her prior reading and independence from it. She has abstracted some elements from her experience of fiction and during the interview she is beginning to think about how she is deploying those elements in her writing.

Teacher: How did you plan your story?
Gemma: Err, well I sort of – you mean apart from the splatter diagrams and that?
Teacher: Yes.
Gemma: Yeah, well, from books and TV and that. Err, I sort of like decided that, you know if these books were good then I've got to have something from these books to make mine good. Sort of like, the idea, and having something from them.

Teacher: How did you know which bits were good, and which bits to use?

Gemma: Urm, well, you don't want to read about people washing their socks and stuff. You know, 'He came downstairs and put his socks in the washer.' You think 'Oh great, yeah.' So put in another bit where you read, like, you know, 'He rolled the stone off the front of the cave and there he saw . . .' You know, you think 'Arrgghh, what did he see, what did he see?' And that gets you involved.

This process seems to operate over a whole range of levels of ability. It may take place at plot level, as with Russell's borrowing of Sky TV movies, or at the level of lexical juxtaposition as with Gemma below. When pupils read their own texts, they seem to engage with the 'virtual reality' of the text as interactive/participant observers.

Looking again at Gemma's interview, there is a section where the visiting teacher is asking her about the number of times she returns to her text.

Teacher: . . . every time you read it through, did you notice anything different? Or was it the same response from the first time?

Gemma: I think it was er, different. Because the first time you do it you like focus in on one thing. Then the second time you do it on another and so on. I reckon I could read it again and probably still find something wrong with 'em.

Teacher: Um. You say 'wrong'. How would you know it was wrong?

Gemma: Well. Wrong to me. I mean it might be perfectly OK to other people, but I might think it sounds different, not quite right.

Teacher: Could you explain to me why it wouldn't sound right? Could you tell me what you look for when things aren't sounding right?

Gemma: Like if I put, something like, a really big word and then I like put another one, it means sort of different things but there's like a more elaborate word for it. They'll think the big word dwarfs it, and it doesn't sound as effective.

We are learning about Gemma as an interactive reader/writer here, and one of the values of this information lies in its potential for development beyond Gemma's observations about her own text. Some of the transactions which form her response are audible as she wrestles with the explanation of her decision-making, and an outcome of that struggle can be the clarification of those transactions. There is potential for a teacher and pupil working together to extrapolate principles from this now-shared experience and to develop practical skills and further awareness from the discussion. Such discussion can bring implicit knowledge into the light, and can allow a teacher to offer reinforcement to concepts which are half-understood or guessed-at. This process of extrapolation can apply to critical principles as well as principles of composition.

Thinking about talking-about-reading-while-writing

Pupils often say 'It just sounded right' in response to questions about changes to drafts. This refrain may be a non-analytic response, or, to be exact, an initial inability or reluctance to analyse, but it does seem to be a response which is based on prior reading and on a learned sense of appropriateness. Teachers and pupils working from that response to explore 'right sounding' need formative assessment information; test scores do not seem appropriate for such work.

The kind of information which emerges from the interviews discussed in this chapter cannot comfortably be identified as independent 'reading' or 'writing' information: it seems to be about both. In this respect, it is typical of classroom information: context-dependent, qualitative and messy. Authentic assessment – assessment based on responses in naturalistic contexts – and the generation of clear-cut, quantitative data seem often to be in tension.

What is sometimes needed is a means of assessment which acknowledges the inextricability of such complex information. For some purposes, it is not necessary, and it can even be counter-productive, to separate out assessments into the notional components of language skill.

Reflecting upon the statements made by pupils about the changes they have made to their writing is not readily going to yield a score, grade or level, or any quantitative information. Instead of trying to get closer to the reading process, the interview accepts its elusiveness and works by inference. It can only offer formative information, and even then only in a deeply contextualized way; possibly without even allowing transferability of information to other teachers. As such, it is one potential assessment strategy in a battery of such strategies.

Perhaps it would be useful to summarize the purposes to which this kind of assessment information is likely to be put:

Responding – the process by which we feed back information to pupils, a process likely to include elements of target-setting and evaluation. Forms of response include:

- written comments;
- spoken comments;
- written questions;
- spoken questions;
- targets;
- grades and/or levels.

Setting targets – using assessment information to generate an agenda for progress which is shared with the pupils. Some information might be readily related to progress (either generally – like 'I'm sick of reading horror books' in a journal – or specifically, like diagnostic information about, say, miscues).

Evaluating – the process of relating a specific piece of assessment information to one kind of context or another. The context might be the pupil's situation and previous performance and might be more deeply contextualized in a variety of ways.

Reporting (to parents and external agencies) – the process of informing others about pupils' performance, either in the form of verbal reports to parents, records of achievement, interim reports on the conventional model, or teacher assessments.

To fulfil these purposes, teachers have quite a wide range of sources; they have experience and they have records about pupils' reading, including, for instance, diagnostic test results of various kinds, transfer information from previous teachers, pupils' self-assessments in reading journals, and teacher impressions of pupils reading aloud. I make a deliberate distinction here between experience and records in order to draw attention to the qualitative difference between those two types of information. A teacher's experience of a pupil is attenuated when a record is made, and there is further attenuation when that record is summarized as a grade. This can perhaps be seen at its clearest in transfer information between primary/elementary and secondary schools, where a grade has a very different value from a written or verbal report. Where genuine professional communication is needed, communication which will enable the receiving teacher to take up responsibility for the pupil's progress, a grade is almost worthless. Such information is inappropriately summative – too broad, too general, too potentially misleading. Even a full report is not regarded as any kind of replacement for the formation of a teacher's own impression.

Assessment, then, can be seen as a necessary abstraction from the teacher's experience of the pupil. At the first remove from that experience, assessment can be a temporary focus rather than a clear separation of independent qualities. Under these circumstances it will be formative and therefore provisional, and will be characterized by institutional context and by the relationship between pupil and teacher. Recording that assessment increases the distance from the teacher's initial perception of the pupil. Reducing that record to a grade represents a further degree of abstraction. These different levels of abstraction serve radically different purposes, even though they are nominally derived from the same data.

If redrafting is an interactive reading of a pupil's own text and that text emerges from readings of other texts and experiences, then redrafting can be seen as a complex and peculiarly authentic reading development activity, and making a record of that activity yields information of value.

In seeking to add another item to the list of sources of information about pupils available to teachers, I am conscious that there are questions regarding the manageability of all this information. Can this information be readily obtained for all pupils? How much information is desirable, before it becomes unwieldy and counter-productive? The answers to such questions must come from a consideration of the purposes for assessment. I do not want to suggest that some kinds of assessment information are more valuable than other kinds, but to suggest that the purpose to which information is put determines its value. Some kinds of information, and some degrees of richness of information, are more fit for particular purposes than others. It is clear that assessment information becomes inconveniently rich for *reporting* before it ceases to be valuable for *responding*.

I have already noted that the interviews described in this chapter do not readily yield information which is easy to report or to refer to norms of attainment. When the purpose of assessment is to assist or guide progress, though, this information might be regarded as more valuable. That it is overtly subjective, inextricable and messy might reduce its status in an assessment culture which prioritizes convenient summary, but that does not prevent it from potentially enhancing the practice of learners and teachers.

References

Bereiter, C. and Scardamalia, M. (1987) *The Psychology of Written Composition*, Hilldale, New Jersey: Lawrence Erlbaum Associates.

Department for Education (1995) *English in the National Curriculum*, London: HMSO.

Flower, L. (1981) *Problem-Solving Strategies for Writing*, New York: Harcourt Brace Jovanovich.

Rosenblatt, L. (1994) 'The transactional theory of reading and writing', in R. Ruddell, M. Ruddell and H. Singer (eds) *Theoretical Models and Processes of Reading*, Newark, Delaware: International Reading Association.

10

ASSESSING LITERACY AND SPECIAL NEEDS IN SECONDARY SCHOOLS

A case for new paradigms

Graham Frater

This chapter makes a case for new paradigms of literacy assessment for most pupils with special needs in the secondary school and for new courses of action based upon them. It arises partly from a survey I undertook for the Basic Skills Agency in England into the provision for Special Educational Needs (SEN) in secondary schools in England during 1995. The paper also draws, in general terms, on the experience of some 181 secondary school English inspections, consultancy visits, in-service training meetings and conferences in the period 1992 to 1996, from discussions arising from them and from a range of observation and reading over a longer period. The survey was undertaken to assist the Basic Skills Agency to determine how and in what aspects of special needs education it might be best placed to offer targeted assistance to secondary schools.

The fifteen schools visited are for pupils aged 11 to 16 or 18 and all but one were non-selective. The survey schools were drawn from contrasting locations in Warwickshire, Coventry, Birmingham, Leeds, Barnsley, Shropshire, Staffordshire and London. In addition, four local authority units supporting the needs of SEN pupils were also visited. The sampling was designed to include a variety of geographical and social contexts. In each case, a questionnaire was used, lessons were observed and interviews were conducted with SEN Coordinators (SENCOs), heads of English and head teachers.

The survey followed closely upon recent legislation in the UK that places extra obligations for pupils who have Special Educational Needs on all public sector providers of education. In brief, the 1993 Education Act requires the Secretary of State for Education and Employment to issue a Code of Practice which all local education authorities (LEAs) and

171

maintained schools must adhere to. Schools must devise policies for special educational needs, have committee structures that involve all subject teams in the care of the relevant pupils and operate a five-stage model for their support. In particular, pupils' SEN must be identified and assessed; a register of pupils with SEN must be maintained; based upon the assessments, individual education plans (IEPs) must be drafted; and progress must be formally and regularly reviewed. Stages 1 to 3 are school-based: at Stage 1 the principal responsibility for identification and support lies with subject teachers and pastoral staff, while at Stages 2 and 3, the school's special needs team is more centrally involved, though still in partnership with subject and other teams. For a minority of cases, an estimated 2 per cent, Stages 4 or 5 may be invoked; in addition to the school's efforts, the statutory involvement of the LEA will be required and a Statement of Special Educational Need must be drafted for each pupil identified. The nature of LEA support varies widely; it is usually offered by a support unit such as those visited for the survey.

Who has special needs?

Both survey evidence and school inspection reveal that the incidence of pupils receiving help from special needs departments varies greatly across the country; in the survey schools the proportions ranged between 6.8 per cent and 39 per cent of the numbers on a school roll. The obligations to support pupils with special needs are unevenly distributed and accord largely with demographic factors. The heaviest demands for support fall on inner city schools (28.6 per cent and 39 per cent of the rolls in the two inner city schools in the survey); these schools have the most obviously disadvantaged intakes. However, a rural setting is no insulation against special needs. The most deeply rural school in the sample had 22 per cent of its pupils receiving help from the special needs team.

Pupils receiving help mostly cluster in the first three years; numbers fall off after the age of fourteen. This does not necessarily signal satisfactory progress. The availability of help is limited by resources and younger pupils are usually prioritized more highly. Virtually no pupils older than 16 received help from SEN departments in the survey schools, though low-attaining students are certainly to be found re-sitting public examinations and taking vocational courses. None of the SEN departments visited provides help to pupils identified as having outstanding abilities. Indeed, other than by setting according to ability, it is rare for maintained secondary schools to make any formal provision for such pupils.

Among those on the Code's five stages, boys sharply outnumber girls. Across the sample, the proportion of boys varied between 55 per cent and 81 per cent of those receiving help and commonly stood around 70 per cent; indeed, among the clients of special needs teams, a ratio of seven boys to three girls appears to be broadly typical. The highest proportion of boys receiving help was found in the most deeply rural location.

Poor literacy as a special need

Though emotional or behavioural problems and physical handicap were among the reasons for being on a register of special needs, they were often associated with poor literacy, and problem literacy was itself the most common reason for being the client of a special needs department. Problems with numeracy, whilst far from rare, seldom led to the same degree of reliance on the special needs department as literacy and were much less likely to prompt an assessment of SEN.

Most schools noted that they had identified some pupils as needing support which, chiefly owing to the resources available, they were unable to provide. Informal evidence also suggests clearly that different statementing practices obtain in relation to the Code of Practice in different local authorities; in part, these differences are also driven by resources. Thus, a pupil who is placed on Stage 4 or 5 in one authority might not be provided with support at the same level in the next.

Special needs teams are staffed by a mixture of qualified teachers and classroom assistants. There was no clear pattern determining either the size of the SEN teams across the schools in the sample, or the balance between qualified teachers and classroom assistants within them. In most schools (84 per cent in the survey), at least one SEN teacher has additional qualifications in the teaching of special needs pupils: these specialist qualifications range from an Open University master's degree in SEN to a local authority's own certificate.

In some local authorities the support team provides teachers or classroom assistants for SEN pupils at Stages 4 and 5 on the register of special needs. All the support teams visited provide support for schools with pupils on the Code of Practice register: the character of this support varies widely but all four teams offer programmes of in-service training for the schools on their lists. However, in practice, the principal obligation to support a pupil with SEN often falls on the subject teachers of the mainstream classes to which that pupil is assigned. For much, often most, of a class's subject timetable, SEN pupils will be in attendance without the presence of an additional adult or expert assistance. It was consistently clear that, whether by initial or by in-service training, secondary school subject specialist teachers are substantially underprepared for supporting pupils with basic reading or writing difficulties in their classes. Time for individual attention by the subject teacher is also at a premium and differentiated teaching materials are at an early stage of development, at best.

Diagnosing special needs in literacy

Evidence both from the survey and a range of other sources suggests that the diagnosis of special needs in literacy is a particular weakness of the school system in England and that it is a weakness of long standing. In a recent study of a nationally representative cohort of young adults (their progress has been plotted since birth) Bynner and Steedman reported that:

> Those with poor basic skills at 21 were unlikely to have been regarded as being in need of special educational provision at age 5 or 10.

> More than half, even of those with very low reading skills, were not reported as having received or having needed additional help when at school.

> Thirty-five per cent of those whose reading scores were very low at 21 were seen at 16 as reading impaired; 15 per cent of those, who at 21 had moderately low scores, were seen at 16 as reading impaired. (Bynner and Steedman 1995: 20–23)

Plainly, the majority of young adults with literacy problems were not identified when at school.

Among the diagnoses of those who *are* identified, the evidence of recent Statements of Special Educational Needs and of IEPs suggests that there are many shortcomings. In large measure, while these documents are clear enough that there is a problem, they are question-begging about the character of the problems themselves. Drawn from a variety of sources, the following recent extracts are all too typical:

A   benefits from support in the classroom for academic subjects. . . .
B   has a great problem with academic work.
C   has poor independent verbal recall and her retention of basic phonic skills is variable. . . . She has . . . poor language skills. . . . Her teachers need to be aware of her problems and monitor her progress. . . .
D   . . . low ability generally – not always very well motivated – needs lots of support and encouragement. . . .
E   not very able . . .
F   able but has a specific spelling problem. . . .
G   orally OK but written work weak.

Bluntly, commentaries of this kind fail to be adequately diagnostic; they do not identify a specific problem and cannot, therefore, underpin a clear course of action. It follows that they are also inadequate for gauging progress or for evaluating the effectiveness of any programme of support that has used them as its starting point. Thus, the kind of help needed by *A* is simply not suggested; the extent of *B*'s problem is indicated in broad and emotive terms, but no remedy is offered. For *C*, it is urged that her teachers be aware of and monitor her problems, but those teachers are denied a meaningful indication either of what the problems are, of what exactly might be monitored or how they should help. It is similar with *D, E, F* and *G*; with the first two indeed, diagnosis is hardly attempted. With *F* and *G*, broad areas of difficulty are hinted at, but neither provides a significant basis either for action or the monitoring of progress. There could hardly be a clearer case for new paradigms of assessment for pupils with poor literacy.

A question of progress

The survey explained here was not a statistical exercise; none the less, as the visits accumulated, observation built up to suggest that, when literacy is a pupil's core problem, progress in the secondary school is seldom clear or steady; in particular, progress was rarely found to be rapid. It was rarer still for a pupil's literacy problems to be eliminated altogether. When shared with teachers, these observations seemed to attract agreement; moreover, they match the broad picture derived from inspections and accord with evidence gathered in a recent survey of research findings on the progress of young people who have experienced difficulties with learning to read:

> There is evidence of a strong link between reading difficulties in primary school and subsequently poor employment history in early adult life.

> Research has found that the remediation of reading problems in older children is largely ineffective.
>
> (Sylva and Hurry 1995: 13; 14)

Little seems to have changed: both in the early 1980s and before, Her Majesty's Inspectorate in England were noting that, all too commonly, the child who was a poor reader at the age of 7 was still a poor reader at 16.

An emerging picture

At this point a number of pieces begin to fall into place, but it is no tidy picture that emerges. With wide variations of provision at school and local authority level, problem literacy is the most common trigger for an assessment of SEN; it frequently accompanies other difficulties and boys are far more likely than girls to experience reading problems. It is *not* the case that all those with problems receive help; this is partly owing to resources, but many pupils experiencing difficulties are not recognized as needing assistance. Typically too, the recognition of a literacy problem is not accompanied by a clear or precise account of its character; in turn, this hinders both the provision of an individually differentiated programme of support and its effective monitoring. Moreover, few teachers of mainstream subjects in secondary schools, the front line in supporting SEN pupils, have been trained either in the diagnosis or remediation of problem literacy.

Meanwhile, there is a structural tension between a school's obligation to teach the curriculum subjects and the requirement that it should pay close attention to individual difficulties. That this is a dilemma rooted in current national policy is clearly indicated by an instruction to school inspectors: 'Pupils' access to the National Curriculum should not be compromised by their withdrawal for additional support for any learning difficulties' (Ofsted 1995: 82).

Clearly, there is a conflict of imperatives. I now believe this conflict to be so acute that, combined with the dominant in-class model of support, it may actually be counter-productive. The worse a pupil's literacy problem is, the more disadvantageous this combination is likely to become. The prevailing model makes an address to a pupil's overarching problems depend on the particular obstacles that emerge during the teaching of subjects other than literacy. Thus, the acquisition of secure literacy is rendered incidental to that to which it is supposed to provide access – the cart firmly placed before the horse. Fragmentation is practically guaranteed, but a steadily focused and concentrated approach to the specific weaknesses described (with whatever adequacy) in an IEP, is actively hindered. Although, when adult help is available, the pupil often copes with the demands made upon his (typically) literacy at particular moments, essentially the prevailing regime does not prepare him to be an effective *independent* reader.

New structures and contexts

The secondary school curriculum is predicated on the security of the student's basic literacy; it was not conceived to establish that security, but to build upon and extend it. It is essential, therefore, that weak secondary school readers make rapid progress and become independent as soon as possible. Indeed, their progress in literacy needs to be much faster than their unproblematic peers. However, as the evidence invoked above suggests, the prevailing rules and structures seldom seem to bring this about; indeed, they are hardly calculated to do so.

Reading Recovery, introduced from New Zealand, and Family Literacy, recent intervention projects for younger children, have proved to be extraordinarily effective.[1] Their procedures are exactly the opposite of in-class

---

1 There are many accounts of the effectiveness of Reading Recovery; one of the most exhaustive is the study by Sylva and Hurry (1995); a more narrative account is provided in Reading Recovery in New Zealand (London: Ofsted/HMSO, 1993). The Family Literacy demonstration programmes were evaluated by Brooks, Gorman et al. 1996.

support. Where in-class support for literacy is typically long-term, contingent and diffuse, both these projects are time-limited, intensive and closely focused. Neither project requires extensive periods of withdrawal from ordinary teaching, but withdrawal is essential to both.

The principles they share hold out the best prospect of real progress with older pupils. To combine the parental dimension of Family Literacy with the structures and professional rigour of Reading Recovery may be all the more vital for the secondary school pupil, who inevitably brings with him long experience of reading failure, often accompanied by complicating negative attitudes. However, it will not be sufficient to train specialist teachers to a high level in specific procedures for one-to-one withdrawal lessons. Withdrawal staff need the support of subject teaching colleagues equipped with the professional skills to identify pupils with special needs in literacy, to complement and support in their own teaching the work accomplished in withdrawal and to engage with the specialists in assessing the progress of SEN students.

Changing practice: new paradigms for literacy assessment in secondary schools

'For teachers to be effective agents of assessment, they must have a deep knowledge of the disciplines of reading and writing and an understanding of their own reading and writing' (IRA/NCTE 1994: 28). It is already plain that the diagnosis of problem literacy is a widespread weakness. However, it is not another external instrument, a new formal test, that is needed. The new professional skills envisaged above need to be internalized and to be applied routinely in day-to-day teaching. One of the surest routes to higher achievement lies in helping both specialist SEN staff and subject teachers to develop their perceptions of pupils' difficulties with literacy and to use a common language and system to record their findings. In particular, it is important that teachers be able to distinguish between slips and systematic errors. As a second and major stage, when errors fall into patterns – as they usually do – teachers need to be able to identify and classify those that are specific to their individual pupils.

One of the most frequent criticisms made in school inspection reports concerns a widespread lack of differentiated teaching. Wherever special needs are found, effective differentiation requires a common professional currency. *What is required is not so much new in itself, as new to secondary schools.* What follows is an indication in summary form of some of the practices I believe hold the clue to significant progress.

- An extension of the processes of miscue analysis used to measure progress in reading in the primary school. Errors are not to be regarded as measures of failure; systematically recorded, they may help to establish a clear baseline, to place limits on a problem, to set targets and priorities and to act as milestones on the route to progress.

- For secondary school pupils whose basic reading skills are insecure on entry, the running record, usually associated with the Reading Recovery programme, is likely to be especially useful. It has the virtue of being rapidly administered and may be used as a daily check if necessary.
- The *Primary Language Record* is more comprehensive and includes both a running record and a wide range of contextual and other evidence; its principles and most of its practices are capable of adaptation to match the literacy requirements of SEN pupils in the secondary school.
- Aspects of writing can be approached in a similarly systematic manner so that a path may be traced through what might otherwise seem overwhelming, and progress may be noted with a measure of clarity and assurance. In their evaluation of the Family Literacy demonstration projects Brooks, Gorman et al. (1996) sought to measure the progress in writing of the parents who had participated in the scheme alongside their children. To do so, they used both impression and analytic marking. The analytic system they devised (ibid., pp. 147–52), made use of clear, principled categories (orthographic, stylistic and grammatical conventions) and is readily adapted both for establishing a baseline and measuring progress with secondary-school students with special needs in literacy.

I conclude with two points of principles. First, potentially technical issues, with their accompanying metalanguage, are diagnostic tools for the teacher; they should form no part of a body of content to be taught to the student, least of all to a struggling one. Second, though taxonomies can help the teacher, the associated teaching will have little impact unless it gives primacy to what pupils perceive to be relevant and to the communicative function of language. What is required for the improvement of pupils with special needs is linguistically informed teaching, not the teaching of linguistic terms or concepts, or any other discrete instruction in skills.

References

Abell, S. (1994) *Helping Adults to Spell*, London: Adult Literacy and Basic Skills Unit.

Barrs, M., Ellis, S., Hester, H. and Thomas, A. (1988) *The Primary Language Record, A handbook for teachers*, London: CLPE/ILEA.

Brooks, G., Gorman, T., Harman, D. and Wilkin, A. (1996) *Family Literacy Works*, London: Basic Skills Agency.

Bynner, J. and Steedman, J. (1995) *Difficulties with Basic Skills*, London: Basic Skills Agency.

Department for Education (1994) *Code of Practice on the Identification and Assessment of Special Educational Needs*, London: DfEE.

Hamilton, M. and Stasinopoulos, M. (1987) *Literacy, Numeracy and Adults*, London: Adult Literacy and Basic Skills Unit.

International Reading Association and National Council for Teachers of English (1994) *Standards for the Assessment of Reading and Writing*, Newark DE: IRA/NCTE.

Office for Standards in Education (1995) *Guidance on the Inspection of Secondary Schools.* London: HMSO.

Sylva, K. and Hurry, J. (1995) *Reading Recovery and Phonological Training for Children with Reading Problems, Full Report*, London: School Curriculum and Assessment Authority.

INDEX

JOHN RYLANDS
UNIVERSITY
LIBRARY OF
MANCHESTER